Bond
No.1 for exam success

English
Comprehension
10 Minute Tests

CEM
(Durham University)

10–11 years

OXFORD
UNIVERSITY PRESS

OXFORD
UNIVERSITY PRESS

Great Clarendon Street, Oxford, OX2 6DP, United Kingdom

Oxford University Press is a department of the University of Oxford.
It furthers the University's objective of excellence in research, scholarship,
and education by publishing worldwide. Oxford is a registered trade mark
of Oxford University Press in the UK and in certain other countries

Text © Oxford University Press 2017

Author: Christine Jenkins

The moral rights of the author have been asserted

First published in 2017

British Library Cataloguing in Publication Data
Data available

978-0-19-275939-9

10 9 8 7 6 5 4 3 2 1

Paper used in the production of this book is a natural, recyclable product
made from wood grown in sustainable forests. The manufacturing process
conforms to the environmental regulations of the country of origin.

Printed in China

Acknowledgements

Cover illustration: Lo Cole
Illustrations: Aptara
Page make-up: Aptara

We are grateful for permission to reprint extracts from the following in this book:

Janine Calzini: 'Experience: I own the world's fastest tortoise', *The Guardian*
magazine, 2 Oct 2015, copyright © Guardian News and Media Ltd 2015, 2016,
reprinted by permission of GNM.

Philippa Pearce: *Tom's Midnight Garden* (OUP, 2015), copyright © Oxford University
Press 1958, reprinted by permission of the publisher.

Useful notes

These 10 minute tests are designed to practise the skill of reading a text quickly but efficiently, while also drawing out the key information.

Reading widely and developing a broad vocabulary is a key skill, not only in preparing for the 11+ but also for secondary education in general. Reading and discussing answers is therefore time well spent. Look up new and unfamiliar words in a dictionary and find synonyms in a thesaurus to develop vocabulary skills.

It is important to read all texts through thoroughly once, before attempting to answer the questions.

When starting to answer, scan the text for key words from the question. Use references given, such as line numbers or paragraphs, to locate information.

Quickly read through a paragraph again or skim read to help establish the context and understand a word or phrase.

Speed can be critical in an 11+ situation, so work on reading speed using these texts. Time how long it takes to read one of the texts. Then return to it several weeks later, and read it again. Remember: read in your head, not aloud.

Some texts can be read easily in one reading, but the questions may take longer to answer. This is because it might be harder to locate the information required or you might need to write a longer answer.

Other texts may be more complex, particularly those taken from older, classic fiction. You will need to read them through more than once to fully understand them. In these cases, more multiple-choice type questions are given.

Where multiple-choice questions give several similar answers, begin by eliminating the ones that are definitely wrong. Then scan the text to find the correct section and read it closely, trying to match the meaning of all the words. Often the meaning is inferred from what is written, especially in fiction texts. Look at how actions and thoughts can convey feelings, and at how descriptions can convey mood.

In non-fiction pieces, use organisational devices, such as subheadings, text boxes and bullet points, to help locate information. Skim and summarise what is in each section and look out for details, such as dates, times and places.

Some questions require knowing the meaning of literary and grammatical terms. These are given in the Key words section on page 95.

Enjoy reading a range of texts, not only in this book, but also for pleasure. Find out about new words and different styles of writing. Try to read appropriate texts aimed at a slightly older age group, or texts in different formats, such as articles from newspapers and magazines.

Test 1

Test time: 0   5   10 minutes

Read the text carefully and answer the questions that follow.

Wartime Food: unusual ingredients

During the Second World War, many foods in Britain were rationed. This
was to ensure that limited food supplies were fairly distributed among the
population. The government was keen for everyone to have a nutritious,
although not always exciting, diet to maintain the nation's health. Everyone
had a ration book, which entitled them to certain amounts of rationed   5
foodstuffs at a standard, regulated price. As a result, poorer people could now
afford more essential vitamin- and mineral-rich foods and, despite foodstuffs
such as meat, butter and eggs being significantly limited, the health of the
general public actually improved during this period. Children, pregnant women
and manual workers were given supplementary allowances of certain foods,   10
such as milk, to cater for their extra nutritional needs.

People were also encouraged to grow their own vegetables, which gave them
greater variety in their monotonous diet. In addition, many open areas of
land, such as golf courses, parks and even grass verges, were turned over to
agriculture as part of the 'Dig for Victory' campaign, and this was seen as a   15
valuable and integral part of the war effort.

A special government department, known as the Ministry of Food, produced
advice for households suggesting ways to use their rations to produce
tasty and well-balanced meals. Simple economical recipes were published,
and cookery programmes were broadcast on the radio. Some of these   20
recipes involved substituting scarce or luxury ingredients with more basic
commodities, although this met with varied success. Cake recipes included
advice on how to replace sugar, which was rationed, with 'sweet' vegetables,
such as carrots and parsnips. There were also suggestions on how to use
powdered eggs and biscuits made of mashed potato. One recipe book even   25
contained a recipe for 'mock' goose using pig's offal, which sounds less than
tempting to modern palates.

1   Underline the correct answer from options **a–d**.
    Rationing was introduced:

    a because supplies of some food were scarce

    b to ensure everyone got a share of the food

    c to make sure the population had a nourishing diet

    d all of the above

2 Explain how poorer people benefited from rationing, referring to the text.

1

_____

_____

3 Underline the correct answer from options **a–d**.

Rationing resulted in:

a poorer health   **b** increased cost   **c** better health   **d** more food supplies

4 What does the word 'supplementary' at the end of paragraph one mean?
Underline the correct answer from options **a–e**.

a expensive   **b** extra   **c** special   **d** nutritious   **e** reduced

5 Which **TWO** words tell you that growing your own vegetables was seen as an important part of the war effort?

_____   _____

6 Underline the correct answer from options **a–e**.

According to the text, the Ministry of Food:

a made rules about exactly what the public must eat

b gave the public helpful suggestions for using their rations

c supplied advice about nutritious meals

d all of the above

e some of the above

> **READ CAREFULLY**
> Scan the text to find the words 'Ministry of Food'. When you have located the relevant part, make sure you look at **all** the information very carefully. Remember: one or more than one of the statements in the question may be true.

7 What do the words 'simple' and 'economical' (line 19) suggest about the recipes given?

_____

8 Explain in your own words what the word 'substituting' means in the final paragraph.

_____

9 Give **TWO** examples of foods that were used to replace other ingredients from the information in the final paragraph.

_____

Total 12

Read the text carefully and answer the questions that follow.

What Katy Did at School by Susan Coolidge
Extract from Chapter 1

The summer had been cool; but, as often happens after cool summers, the
autumn proved unusually hot. It seemed as if the months had been playing
a game, and had "changed places" all round; and as if September were
determined to show that he knew how to make himself just as disagreeable as
August, if only he chose to do so. All the last half of Cousin Helen's stay, the   **5**
weather was excessively sultry. She felt it very much, though the children did
all they could to make her comfortable, with shaded rooms, and iced water,
and fans. Every evening the boys would wheel her sofa out on the porch, in
hopes of coolness; but it was of no use: the evenings were as warm as the
days, and the yellow dust hanging in the air made the sunshine look thick and   **10**
hot. A few bright leaves appeared on the trees, but they were wrinkled, and of
an ugly color. Clover said she thought they had been boiled red like lobsters.
Altogether, the month was a trying one, and the coming of October made little
difference: still the dust continued, and the heat; and the wind, when it blew,
had no refreshment in it, but seemed to have passed over some great furnace   **15**
which had burned out of it all life and flavor.

1 Explain in what way the months were 'playing a game'.   ◯ 1

_____

_____

2 Underline the correct answer from options **a–d**.   ◯ 1
The word 'sultry' in line 6 is closest in meaning to:

a hot and dry   **b** humid and oppressive   **c** bright and warm   **d** shady and cool

3 Tick **ALL** that apply.   ◯ 3
The children helped to keep Cousin Helen cool by:

a providing shade   ☐   **b** sitting on the sofa with her   ☐

c making sure she had cold drinks   ☐   **d** taking her outside in the evening   ☐

4 Underline the correct answer from options **a–d**. ⬜ 1

The trees had:

a no leaves   **b** green leaves   **c** small leaves   **d** withered leaves

5 Complete the following sentence using a **FOUR**-letter word, based on the information in the text. ⬜ 1

__ __ __ __ hung in the air.

6 Find a word in the text that shows that the weather in September tested everyone's patience. ⬜ 1

_____

7 Which word in the text means an enclosed chamber that heats things to a high temperature? ⬜ 1

_____

8 Beside each of the following statements, tick **ONE** box to show whether it is **TRUE** or **FALSE**. ⬜ 1

	TRUE	FALSE
a In October, the weather stayed hot.		
b In October, there was a refreshing breeze.		
c October was a very windy month.		
d There was no improvement in the dusty atmosphere in October.		

9 Use a line to match each literary device to the example from the text. ⬜ 3

a boiled red like lobsters   personification

b he knew how to make himself just as disagreeable as August   description

c excessively sultry   simile

> **PERSONIFICATION**
> Personification is when something that is not human is given human actions and characteristics. To spot personification, look for pronouns such as 'he', 'she', 'his' and 'her' instead of 'it' and 'its'. Look also for verbs that denote human actions, for example, 'The wind sang.'

Total ⬜ 13

Test 3

Read the text carefully and answer the questions that follow.

Rainforest Blog

Jen Hawkins is an animal behaviour expert who is studying some of the species in the Amazon rainforest. Here is her blog.

Friday, 12th May

We've arrived in Brazil at last. I can't believe I am finally here. From the airport, we took a taxi to the city of Manaus where I met up with my local guide,   **5**
Carlito. He was born and raised in the Amazon rainforest and will be travelling with me, helping to keep me safe. We will stay in a treehouse hotel tonight and set off deeper into the forest in the morning. I can't wait to see some of the amazing animals I've been studying in their natural habitat.

Saturday, 13th May   **10**

We took a motorboat along the vast Amazon river this morning. As we got further away from civilisation, the vegetation became denser and we had to wind our way through the overhanging branches. Carlito told me to look out for pink dolphins in the water and before long I caught my first glimpse. What a sight!   **15**

After four hours, we found a flat clearing, close to the river – the ideal spot to set up camp. Carlito showed me how to build a shelter and light a fire, using the many fallen branches all around. It wasn't long before we had company: a group of woolly monkeys appeared in the branches beside our camp. Watching them play around among the branches was hilarious. Some even   **20**
came close to us and took a banana! The heat and humidity is intense here, which can be pretty exhausting. As darkness falls, I listen to the sounds of the forest all around. What an amazing and memorable first day I've had.

Monday, 15th May

Since I last blogged, I've learnt from Carlito how to find forest fruits that are   **25**
safe to eat and how to fish for piranhas using a wooden spear. I can't believe the number of different animals I've seen: parrots, tree frogs and even a sloth. I've realised that even the smallest creatures need to be respected. One sting or bite from some of these tiny insects can cause extreme pain or even prove fatal. Luckily, Carlito knows exactly where to find areas where we are less   **30**
likely to be bitten. Tomorrow is our last day in this incredible environment. There is no place on Earth like it and I'm leaving with a new understanding of animal behaviour and with memories that will last a lifetime.

1 Find **TWO** phrases or sentences in the first entry of her blog that show that Jen is feeling excited and incredulous about being there. Write them below.

FINDING WORDS
To find out about someone's feelings, scan the text for the pronouns 'I' and 'me', and then read on.

(2)

_____

_____

2 Read the blog entry for Saturday, 13th May. Which word shows that the Amazon is a big river?

(1)

_____

3 Underline the correct answer from options **a–d** to complete the sentence.

(1)

The river became more overgrown with plants as they got further away from:

a people and buildings **b** the equator **c** the airport **d** Carlito's home town

4 Which of the following is closest in meaning to 'vegetation' in line 12? Underline the correct answer.

(1)

a plant life **b** vegetables **c** treetops **d** plant-eating

5 Two of the following reasons are false. Underline the **TWO** that are **TRUE**.

(2)

It was a good place to set up camp because:

a there was a space with no trees **b** it was far away from the river

c it was on a slope **d** there was plenty of wood around

6 From the evidence throughout Jen's blog, how do we know Carlito does his job well?

(3)

_____

_____

_____

7 Write **F** or **O** to show whether the following statements are **F**acts or **O**pinions.

(1)

a Woolly monkeys are funny. _____

b Not all forest fruits are safe to eat. _____

c Some insect bites can kill you. _____

d Pink dolphins are beautiful to look at. _____

Time for a break! ★ Go to Puzzle Page 86 →

Total   11

Read the text carefully and answer the questions that follow.

How Viking Sagas Began

Iceland is a little country far north in the cold sea. Men from Norway
discovered it and went to live there more than a thousand years ago. During
the warm season, they used to fish, produce fish oil, hunt seabirds, gather
feathers, tend their sheep and make hay. But the winters were long, dark and
cold. A whole family would sit for hours around the fire in the middle of the   **5**
room, spinning, weaving and knitting. That fire gave the only light. Shadows
flitted in the dark corners and smoke curled along the high beams in the
ceiling. The children sat on the dirt floor close by the fire; the adults sat on a
long narrow bench. Everybody's hands were busy with wool. The work left
their minds free to think and their lips to talk. They talked about the summer's   **10**
fishing, the killing of a fox, a voyage to Norway. But the people grew tired
of this. Fathers looked at their children and thought: "They are not learning
much. What will make them brave and wise and teach them to love their
country and old Norway? Will not the stories of battles, of brave deeds, of
mighty men, do this?"   **15**

So, as the family worked in the red firelight, the father told of the kings of
Norway, of long voyages to strange lands, of good fights. And in farmhouses
all through Iceland, these old tales were told over and over until everybody
knew them and loved them. Some men could sing and play the harp. People
called such men 'skalds', and they called their songs 'sagas'.   **20**

For many years, these tales were not written down, since few people wrote or
read in those days. Skalds learnt songs from hearing them sung. When at last
people began to write more easily, they said: "These stories are precious. We
must write them down to save them from being forgotten."

So they spent their winters recording these ancient tales, writing on sheepskin   **25**
pages known as vellum. Many of these precious old vellum books have been
saved for hundreds of years, and are now in museums in Norway, telling about
a time long ago – stories of kings, battles and ship-sailing.

Taken from Viking Tales *by Jennie Hall, adapted by Christine Jenkins*

1 Underline the correct answer.

In paragraph one, the phrase 'shadows flitted' suggests they:

a moved slowly   **b** darted about   **c** disappeared   **d** hovered in the corner

2 Using the information in paragraph one, tick next to each statement to show whether it is **TRUE** or **FALSE**.

	TRUE	FALSE
a It is never warm in Iceland.		
b On winter evenings, the only light came from the fire.		
c Iceland is a long way north.		
d It took lots of concentration to spin, weave and knit.		

3 Which of the following were reasons the fathers started to tell stories to their children? Tick **ALL** the options that are **TRUE**.

a They wanted them to learn how to hunt. ☐

b They knew the children had already learnt about their heroes. ☐

c They wanted them to find out more about some Norwegian legends. ☐

d They wanted to inspire them to be courageous. ☐

e They wanted them to stop sitting by the fire. ☐

4 Find **ONE** word from the text for each of the meanings below.

a A long sea journey _____

b Writing down _____

c An instrument played by the men who sang the sagas _____

5 Why did people at first learn the sagas from hearing them sung?

_____

6 Why do you think the tales were not told during the warmer weather?

_____

7 Name **TWO** ways the early Icelandic settlers used their sheep.

_____

_____

Total 11

Test 5

Read the text carefully and answer the questions that follow.

The Traveller's Purse

One day, two young men were travelling along the road together when one of them spotted a purse bulging with coins, lying by the verge. Quick as a wink, he picked it up.

"How lucky I am!" he boasted. "I have found a purse. Judging by its weight, it must be full of gold." **5**

"Do not say '*I* have found a purse'," said his fellow traveller, looking on in envy. "Instead you should say '*we* have found a purse' and 'how lucky *we* are'. We are companions after all. Companions ought to share alike the fortunes or misfortunes of the road."

"No chance. Why should I share it?" replied the other indignantly. "*I* found it and *I* am going to keep it." **10**

Just then, they heard a shout of "Stop, thief!" and, looking around, saw an angry mob of people armed with clubs coming down the road towards them.

Realising they were after him, the man who had found the purse fell into a panic.

"We are lost if they find the purse on us," he cried, grabbing his companion and trying to hide the purse from the approaching crowd. **15**

"No, no," replied the other. "You would not say 'we' before, so now stick to your 'I'. Say '*I* am lost'." And with that, he pulled away, leaving his fellow traveller to his fate.

Moral: We cannot expect anyone to share our misfortunes unless we are also **20**
willing to share our good fortune.

---

1 Complete the paragraph below, using **ONE** word from the box in each space. (8)

cash	side	throng	gloated
noticed	split	companion	purse

Travelling along one day, a young man _____ a _____

at the _____ of the road. He _____ about finding

it and refused to _____ the _____ with his

_____. When an angry _____ pursued him, however,

his fellow traveller got his own back.

Select the **ONE** word from options **a–e** that is **OPPOSITE** in meaning to the given word from the text. Underline the correct answer.

2 together

   a near   **b** close   **c** beside

   d apart   **e** often

> ## EXPERIMENTING WITH WORDS
> When looking for words with the opposite meaning (antonyms), try putting each of the alternative words into a sentence and seeing if it changes the meaning to the direct opposite.

3 misfortune

   a hardship   **b** sadness   **c** treasure

   d happiness   **e** luck

4 shout

   a speak   **b** whisper   **c** call   **d** cry   **e** sing

5 Underline the correct answer.

The use of the word 'indignantly' in the text (line 10) shows that the traveller:

   a knew he was wrong

   b didn't like his companion

   c thought it was unfair to expect the money to be shared

   d was keen to set off

6 In line 15, what does the man mean when he says "we are lost if they find the purse on us"?

_____

7 What does the use of the word 'approaching' in line 16 show the reader about the crowd?

_____

8 Complete both the following words from the text, using the same **THREE**-letter word.

   __ __ __ IC   COM __ __ __ ION

9 Explain why the use of the pronouns 'I' and 'we' is important in the story.

I: _____

We: _____

3

1

1

1

1

2

Total 17

13

Read the two texts below and answer the questions that follow.

Titanic **Fact File**

Most people have heard of *Titanic* and know something about the fateful story of its maiden voyage in 1912. There are many interesting facts, figures and stories about the ship and the disaster that unfolded.

Did You Know?

- *Titanic* had a sister ship called *Olympic*. They were built side by side in Belfast.   5

- One stewardess on board, Violet Jessop, survived not only the *Titanic* disaster but also the sinking of another ship, *Britannic*, on which she later worked.

- Some passengers had brought their pets on board and, when the ship hit the iceberg, at least two dogs survived: a Pomeranian and a Pekinese.

- There was a Post Office on board *Titanic*; many sacks of mail were lost with   10
the ship.

- The *Titanic* disaster led the way for improvements in ships' safety, especially regulations requiring a greater number of lifeboats.

- *Titanic* had four funnels, but only three were actually used. The fourth was only for show.

   15

A Taste of History

Studying the menus that have survived from *Titanic* can give us a small insight into life on board. For passengers travelling first class, food on board would have rivalled the finest French restaurants. Salmon, oysters and roast duckling all featured in one ten-course dinner and, even in second class, the variety and quality of food was reported to be significantly better than on other ships of the time. Third-class passengers were   5
not catered for quite so luxuriously, although they are not likely to have gone hungry; their dinner menu included roast beef and gravy with boiled potatoes, as well as cabin biscuits. The ongoing fascination with the story of *Titanic* means artefacts, such as menus, are highly valuable. In 2015, a menu from the last lunch served on board, which had been saved by a surviving first-class passenger, was sold for over £58 000. It   10
included grilled mutton chops, apple meringue and several types of cheese. Perhaps one of the most eerie sights related to *Titanic* is that of the thousands of fine plates and dishes that had sunk to the bottom of the ocean with the ship, photographed many years later by submersibles sent down to investigate the wreck.

1   When did *Titanic* first sail?

_____

2 Find **TWO** words in the opening paragraph of '*Titanic* Fact File' that indicate something bad happened to *Titanic*.

_____   _____

3 Put a tick next to each of the statements to indicate if it is **TRUE** or **FALSE**.

	TRUE	FALSE
a *Titanic* was the only ship of its kind at the time.		
b There were no survivors when *Titanic* sank.		
c Letters waiting to be sent by passengers were saved.		
d Violet Jessop survived two shipping disasters.		
e More lifeboats were required after the disaster.		

4 *Titanic*'s menus are historically as well as financially valuable. Explain how this statement is true, with reference to 'A Taste of History'.

Historically valuable: _____

Financially valuable: _____

5 Select the meaning that is closest to the following phrase from 'A Taste of History'. Underline the correct answer from options **a–d**.

'rivalled the finest French restaurants' suggests that:

a food in first class was always French

b French restaurants were trying to compete with *Titanic*

c All *Titanic*'s chefs were French

d the food in first class was as good as the best restaurants in France

Find the word in 'A Taste of History' with the same meaning as each of the following words.

6 knowledge _____

7 creepy _____

8 examine _____

9 underwater vehicle _____

Total 10

Test 7

Read the text carefully and answer the questions that follow.

Strange Changes: how the peppered moth has adapted

The story of the peppered moth is an amazing example of how animals can adapt, over time, to survive in different surroundings. Prior to the Industrial Revolution at the end of the 18th century, this fascinating British insect was predominantly white with black speckles (hence its name), although a small number of moths had darker markings. The lighter-coloured variety was   **5** better camouflaged against the white tree bark and lichens in the woodlands where it lived. Consequently, this variety was less likely to be spotted and eaten by predators.

The invention of machines to carry out many manufacturing processes during the Industrial Revolution resulted in increasing numbers of factories, which   **10** produced vast amounts of black smoke from their chimneys. The soot in the air caused the discolouration of trees and killed the lichen in the area, against which the darker-coloured variety of moths were better camouflaged, making them less vulnerable to predators. As more of them survived and reproduced, this darker-coloured strain of the peppered moth became the more common type.   **15** By 1898, scientists had calculated that 98% of the peppered moths in some areas were black.

In the mid-20th century, new laws were put in place to improve air quality, resulting in less pollution, and trees were therefore no longer covered with sooty deposits. The lighter variants of the peppered moth survived in this habitat better,   **20** again because of the camouflage afforded by their colouring. By the end of the century, the moth population became predominantly lighter in colour again.

This amazing story of how a creature's appearance has changed over time to survive better within a particular environment is one of the best-known examples of natural selection the world over.   **25**

1 Tick **ALL** the statements that are **TRUE**.

Before the Industrial Revolution:

    a all peppered moths were pale with black speckles ☐

    b the majority of peppered moths were pale with black speckles ☐

    c a few peppered moths were darker ☐

    d darker-coloured peppered moths were well camouflaged ☐

2 In paragraph two, what does the word 'vast' mean? Explain in your own words.   1

_____

3 Complete the paragraph below, using **ONE** word from the box in each space.   8

pollution	machinery	coated	noticeable
factories	soot	prevalent	prey

During the Industrial Revolution, many _____ were built, containing

newly invented _____. Unfortunately, these often caused

_____, which resulted in trees becoming _____

in a layer of _____. The change in surroundings meant that

lighter-coloured moths were more _____, which made them easy

_____. The darker moths became more _____.

4 What reason does the author give for the reduction in pollution in the latter half of the 20th century?   1

_____

Select the **ONE** word on the right that has the most **SIMILAR** meaning to the word on the left. Underline the correct answer.   2

5 calculated   **a** decided   **b** assessed   **c** predicted   **d** observed   **e** thought

6 predominantly   **a** mainly   **b** liberally   **c** unusually   **d** often   **e** only

Total   14

Read the text carefully and answer the questions that follow.

John Cage: the man who composed silence

Have you ever stopped and listened? It is surprising how many sounds we can actually hear when we think there is silence. Silence, or the absence of sound, became regarded as an element of music by many composers in the 20th century. An American composer named John Cage took this to the extreme in his most famous piece, known as *4'33"*, composed in 1952.   5

John Cage was born in Los Angeles in 1912 and studied with many renowned modern composers of the time. However, he soon began to experiment. He was interested in pushing the boundaries of what was considered to be music and he explored the role of chance in composition. He enjoyed using newly created electronic musical devices, as well as resources not traditionally   10 considered to be instruments, including tin cans. He even composed music that created incidental percussion sounds, produced by putting a range of objects (made of rubber, metal and wood) on the strings of a piano. However, he is perhaps best known for his composition *4'33"*.

4'33" is a sound experiment, which consists of a musical score for one   15 or more instruments. The score directs the performers not to play their instruments for four minutes and 33 seconds. Although it is sometimes thought of as silence, Cage claimed the 'piece' is created by whatever noises are heard in the environment for the duration of the four and a half minutes. The piece will therefore change every time it is performed. It illustrates   20 perfectly Cage's belief that any sound could be considered music. He believed it was his most important work.

So, next time you are sitting quietly and you think it is silent, try listening carefully for four and a half minutes. It may surprise you just how much you can hear!

1 How did some composers in the 20th century define silence?   1

_____

2 Which statement best fits John Cage? Underline the correct answer.   1

a He preferred silence to noise.

b He enjoyed being inventive with his music.

c He only composed music for electronic instruments.

d He did not want to study music.

e He thought a noisy environment spoilt the silence.

3 Why are inverted commas used for the term 'piece' in line 18?

1

_____

Select the **ONE** word on the right that has the most **SIMILAR** meaning to the word on the left. Underline the correct answer.

2

4 duration   **a** beat   **b** total   **c** distance   **d** piece   **e** time

5 renowned   **a** acclaimed   **b** amazing   **c** experimental   **d** fashionable   **e** beloved

These sentences have been jumbled up and all have **ONE** extra word. Underline the word that is not needed.

2

6 born in composed was America Cage

7 the not their performers do play in piece sounds the instruments

The following sentences have **ONE** word missing. Complete the sentences by selecting and underlining a word from options **a–e**.

2

8 Every _____ of John Cage's most famous composition is different.

   a piece

   b score

   c silence

   d performance

   e instrument

9 John Cage gave _____ instructions to performers in his most famous piece.

   a vague

   b unusual

   c no

   d complicated

   e many

Total   9

Test 9

Read the text carefully and answer the questions that follow.

Letter of Complaint

Dear Restaurant Manager

Last Friday night, I had the misfortune to dine in your restaurant 'The Harvest Mouse' with my elderly parents, to celebrate my mother's 80th birthday. Our visit did not get off to a good start: not only were we left waiting in the draughty porch area for at least ten minutes before a member of staff noticed that we had arrived, but the waiter could find no record of my booking when he looked. 5

Having finally been taken to a table, we perused the seemingly extensive menu. However, it appeared that, unfortunately, the reality was somewhat different. Our waitress informed us that two of the five starters were unavailable and, when we ordered new potatoes, we were told that only chips were available that evening. After another lengthy wait, our food appeared. To say that my meal looked unappealing is an understatement. The gravy was cold and congealed, the vegetables were soft and grey, and the meat had the appearance of worn leather. My father's steak looked no more appetising. Despite having asked for it to be well done, it arrived looking almost raw. We asked the waiter to take the meals back but, by the time new meals arrived, my mother had finished her main course. It was hardly conducive to an enjoyable meal. 10 15

The desserts were admittedly much better but, in the time it took for them to come, I could have popped to the supermarket, bought the ice cream myself and arrived back in time to serve it! 20

On mentioning our complaints as we paid the bill, the staff were rude and unhelpful, even pulling faces behind our backs. I would appreciate a full apology and would welcome your thoughts on how you will compensate for our disappointing visit. I would also recommend better staff training in dealing with customers. I look forward to your written reply. 25

Yours faithfully

Coral Jones (Miss)

---

1   Which word in line 2 indicates that the restaurant visit did not go well?

_____

2 What **TWO** complaints does Coral Jones make about the restaurant before she and her parents were seated?

_____

_____

2

3 Select the **ONE** word on the right that has the most **SIMILAR** meaning to the word on the left. Underline the correct answer.

perused   **a** ate   **b** chose   **c** glanced   **d** examined   **e** ordered

4 Cross out the incorrect word or words in brackets and give a reason from the text to complete the sentence.

The range of food available (was/was not) extensive because _____

_____

5 Give **TWO** adjectives used to describe the food in lines 13–16.

_____

6 Read the following paragraph and add **ONE** word from the box to each space so that the paragraph makes sense. Each word can only be used once.

staff	slow	impolite	better	disappointed

The desserts were _____ than the main

course, although the experience was spoilt by the

service being _____. When Coral Jones

paid the bill, she told the _____ that

she was _____, but their response was

_____.

> **GRAMMATICAL CLUES**
>
> When completing sentences with missing words, look for clues to work out the kind of word needed. For example, if the sentence starts with a noun phrase 'The terrible food ...', a verb will probably be needed next.

7 What does Coral hope the manager will do in response to her letter? Underline **THREE** answers from options **a–e**.

a write to her parents   **b** say sorry   **c** invite them back

d offer compensation   **e** train the staff

Total 13

Test 10

Read the text carefully and answer the questions that follow.

Keeping Dry: a short history of the umbrella

The first umbrellas appeared almost 4000 years ago in ancient Egypt. They were made from palm leaves and were used to provide shade from the fierce Egyptian sun. In fact, the word 'umbrella' comes from the Latin word 'umbra' meaning 'shade'. Nowadays, we may take this everyday item for granted but, when they were first invented, umbrellas or parasols were a sign of privilege and were only used by the rich and powerful, such as royalty and religious leaders. Evidence for this is found in paintings and carvings from many ancient Egyptian ruins, depicting pharaohs and priests being covered by sunshades held by slaves. By the 11th century, the Chinese had come up with the idea of creating waterproof umbrellas to provide protection from the rain. These were made by covering the paper shades with wax and they usually had a wooden handle.

5

10

It was not long before the umbrella came to Europe, where it was primarily a female accessory for many years. Not until a prominent man called Jonas Hanway started using his umbrella frequently in public did it become fashionable for men to use them. In fact, gentlemen's umbrellas were known as 'Hanways' for many years. Further innovation in the 20th century led to the invention of the folding collapsible umbrella and the lightweight items we have today.

15

Now affordable and available for anyone, umbrellas can be found in every high street, with all manner of patterns and colours. Modern inventors have tried their best to improve the basic design of the umbrella, including providing a spy hole in the hood, and adding anything from cup-holders to golf clubs in the handle. The end result is never too far away, however, from those palm branches on sticks used by the ancient Egyptians!

20

25

1 Complete the following sentence by selecting **ONE** of options **a–e** that is the best fit. Underline your answer.

The earliest umbrellas were:

a used only by women   **b** not used by ordinary people   **c** of religious importance

d an everyday item   **e** made from waxed paper

2 Explain what improvements the Chinese made to the design and usefulness of umbrellas.

Design: _____

Usefulness:_____

3 How do historians know about ancient Egyptian umbrellas?

_____

4 Select the **ONE** word on the right that has the most **SIMILAR** meaning to the word on the left, from line 12 in the text. Underline the correct answer.

primarily   **a** completely   **b** firstly   **c** mainly   **d** especially   **e** noticeably

5 Select the **ONE** word on the right that is most **OPPOSITE** in meaning to the word on the left, from line 14 in the text. Underline the correct answer.

fashionable   **a** beautiful   **b** ugly   **c** old   **d** outdated   **e** stylish

6 Read the following paragraph and add **ONE** word from the box to each space so that the paragraph makes sense. There are more words than there are spaces so some will be left out, but each word can only be used once.

expensive   affordable   hood   handle   design   purchased   invented

Nowadays, a wide range of umbrellas can be easily _____ for an

_____ price. Although the _____ is still similar to

the earliest umbrellas, new innovations have included various additions to the

_____ and space to see out of the _____.

Total 11

Test 11

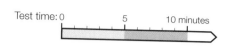

Read the text carefully and answer the questions that follow.

The Dog and His Reflection

Once there was a stray dog who thought himself astute, although in fact the opposite was true. One day, this dog, to whom the generous butcher had thrown a bone, was hurrying home with his prize as fast as he could go. As he crossed a narrow footbridge over the river, he happened to look down: he could hardly believe his eyes! Reflected in the quiet water, as if in a mirror, he saw himself. However, the greedy dog did not understand; he thought he saw a real dog carrying a bone much bigger than his own. His mouth watered as he dreamed of gnawing that juicy bone. Surely it would not be too hard to snatch the bone from the other mangy-looking dog? **5**

If he had stopped to think, he would have known better. But instead of thinking, he dropped his bone into the water and sprang at the dog in the river, only to find himself swimming for dear life to reach the shore. He splashed and floundered, struggling to keep his head above water, while the other dog was nowhere to be seen. At last, he managed to scramble out, and as he stood sadly thinking about the good bone he had lost, he realised his mistake. What a stupid dog he had been! **10** **15**

Moral: It is very foolish to be greedy.

> ## MAKING DEDUCTIONS
> A fable is a traditional kind of story that tries to give a message from which the reader might learn. This is called a 'moral'. To understand the moral of the story fully, look at what goes wrong and why this happens. What should the main character have done instead? Making these deductions will help you answer questions about the text more easily.

1 Underline the best answer from options **a–e**.

The dog had a bone because:

a he had won a prize   **b** he was clever   **c** he had begged for it

d he was in a hurry   **e** he had been given it

2 Select the **ONE** word on the right that is most **OPPOSITE** in meaning to the word on the left, as used in line 4 of the text. Underline the correct answer.

narrow   **a** small   **b** tight   **c** wide   **d** big   **e** overgrown

3 Read the following paragraph and add **ONE** word from the box to each space so that the paragraph makes sense. There are more words than there are spaces so some will be left out, but each word can only be used once.

another	confused	reflection	jealous	own
larger	special	mirror	jumped	stray

The dog saw his own _____ in the river, but was _____.

Thinking he had seen _____ dog, he was _____ of

the dog's _____ bone. He _____ into the water but, in

doing so, lost his _____ bone.

4 Explain what is meant by the phrase 'swimming for dear life' in line 12.

_____

5 This sentence has been jumbled up and has **ONE** extra word. Underline the word that is not needed.

foolish the jumped the dog water into bone

6 Underline the correct answer from options **a–d**.

The phrase 'at last, he managed to scramble out' (line 14) shows that:

a it was difficult with the bone in his mouth

b he was trying to get to the other dog

c he wasn't a good swimmer

d it was difficult to climb out of the water

7 Read the following descriptions and decide which **TWO** best fit the dog in the story. Underline the correct answers from options **a–d**.

a a greedy dog who wanted more

b an angry dog who attacked another

c a lazy dog who stole a bone

d a covetous dog who learnt his lesson

Total 14

Test 12

Read the text carefully and answer the questions that follow.

Unusual Islands

Recent advances in satellite technology have allowed the world's surface to be photographed from space as never before, giving us a bird's-eye view of the land below. This has revealed the unusual shape of many islands, some of which look uncannily like different objects when viewed from above.

Isabela Island, Ecuador

5

Situated off the northwestern coast of South America, Isabela Island belongs to a group of islands called the Galapagos. Isabela is thought to have been formed from six volcanoes joining together, and is one of the most volcanically active places in the world. The lava creates rich fertile soil, producing abundant vegetation. Most strikingly, the island is shaped like a seahorse. Isabela lies directly on the equator and, when viewed on a map, the equator runs straight through the 'head' of the seahorse.

10

Galesnjak, Croatia

Almost a perfect heart shape, this island has become known as 'Lovers' Island' for obvious reasons. Despite being uninhabited and rather barren, its unspoilt landscape and lack of man-made facilities seem to have added to its appeal as the ideal romantic place to visit.

15

Flores Island, Indonesia

What could be more beautiful than a coral reef island shaped like a dolphin? That is what tourists can see off the north coast of Flores. Another volcanic island, near the popular destination of Bali, Flores is increasingly attracting visitors and it is not hard to see why: unspoilt villages, lush forests, picture-perfect beaches and smouldering volcanos all appeal to holidaymakers. The lucky ones may even see one of the island's Komodo dragons!

20

Complete the following sentences by selecting, from options **a–e**, the ending that is the best fit. Underline your answer.

1 According to the first paragraph in the text, satellite technology has helped:

  a to reveal previously undiscovered islands

  b to show the shape of some islands more clearly

  c to view birds from above

  d to take photographs of space

  e with photographing different objects

2 According to the second paragraph in the text, Isabela Island:

a was once a single volcano

b is near the Galapagos Islands

c is one of six islands

d is part of mainland South America

e is in a volcanic area

Select the **ONE** word on the right that has the most **SIMILAR** meaning to the words on the left, taken from the text. Underline the correct answer.

2

3 thrive   **a** climb   **b** dwindle   **c** reproduce   **d** flourish   **e** attach

4 situated   **a** formed   **b** seen   **c** located   **d** put   **e** viewed

Select the **ONE** word on the right that has the most **OPPOSITE** meaning to the words on the left, taken from the text. Underline the correct answer.

3

5 lush   **a** uninhabited   **b** beautiful   **c** abundant   **d** fertile   **e** barren

6 man-made   **a** busy   **b** quiet   **c** unique   **d** natural   **e** attractive

7 uninhabited   **a** populated   **b** dense   **c** appealing   **d** popular   **e** tourist

Find the missing **THREE** letters that complete these words. The three letters must make a word. The same three letters are used for both words.

2

8 UN _ _ _ NILY   VOL _ _ _ IC

9 UNSP _ _ _ T   S _ _ _

4

10 List **FOUR** things that may make the island of Flores appeal to tourists.

_____

_____

_____

_____

Total   13

Test 13

Read the text carefully and answer the questions that follow.

Trolls: creatures from folk tales
What is a troll?
Trolls are ugly mythical creatures found in Scandinavian folklore.

Where did they originate?
Many years ago, the Norse people, who lived in countries around northern
Germany and Scandinavia (Denmark, Finland, Norway and Sweden), had their   **5**
own set of beliefs and stories known as Norse mythology. Trolls feature in
many of these tales.

What are they like?
Trolls are usually described as being either dwarves or giants, with long
prominent noses and grotesque brutish features. Their bodies are often   **10**
depicted covered in long wild hair and they have sharp teeth or even tusks. In
most stories, trolls are rude and aggressive towards others, especially humans.

Where do they live?
In many traditional tales, trolls dwell in dark, dank caves or among the craggy
rocks in the mountains. Some stories involve them living in castles and   **15**
coming out to roam the grounds at night.

What do they do?
Trolls are usually depicted as unpleasant grumpy creatures who try to harm
humans, although in many tales the humans outwit the trolls in the end. Even
their name, in ancient Norse, is another word for 'evil'.   **20**

Perhaps the most famous troll of all is the one in the tale of the *Three Billy
Goats Gruff*. He lives under a bridge, threatening to eat each billy goat as it
crosses his bridge. In the end, the clever goats outsmart him by promising
that a bigger and better goat will come along next. The troll is no match for the
final billy goat and ends up being tossed in the water.   **25**

---

1 Complete the sentence by selecting from options **a–e**. Underline your answer.   1

Trolls are:

a real creatures found in Norway

b small furry animals

c an ancient group of people from Germany

d modern fictional characters

e fabled creatures found in myths from Scandinavia

2 List **FIVE** aspects of a troll's **APPEARANCE** that are described in the text.

_____

_____

_____

_____

_____

3 In most folk tales, where do trolls live?

_____

4 Choose a reason from options **a–e**. Underline your answer.

The name 'troll' is a suitable one because:

a they are tall creatures with long noses

b their name, in the old Norse language, reflects their behaviour towards humans

c they send people nasty messages and try to outwit them

d they live under bridges

e it is an ancient Norwegian word for dwarf

Select the **TWO** odd words out on each line. Select your answers by underlining **TWO** of the options **a–e**.

5 **a** threaten   **b** bully   **c** grumble   **d** intimidate   **e** outsmart

6 **a** aggressive   **b** famous   **c** angry   **d** ugly   **e** hostile

7 Explain what the words 'The troll is no match for the final billy goat' in lines 24–25 mean.

_____

_____

Test 14

Read the text carefully and answer the questions that follow.

The Brook by C. C. Long
    From a fountain
    In a mountain,
  Drops of water ran
Trickling through the grasses;
    So our brook began.   **5**

    Slow it started;
    Soon it darted,
  Cool and clear and free,
Rippling over pebbles,
    Hurrying to the sea.   **10**

    Children straying
    Came a-playing
  On its pretty banks;
Glad, our little brooklet
    Sparkled up its thanks.   **15**

    Blossoms floating,
    Mimic boating,
  Fishes darting past,
Swift, and strong, and happy,
    Widening very fast.   **20**

    Bubbling, singing,
    Rushing, ringing,
  Flecked with shade and sun.
Soon our pretty brooklet
    To the sea has run.   **25**

1   Where does the brook start?

_____

2   Find **THREE** prepositions in verse one.

_____

> ## PREPOSITIONS
> Prepositions are words that show the relationship between a noun or pronoun and another part of the sentence. Examples include 'below' and 'over'.

3 Read the following paragraph and add **ONE** word from the list to each space so that the paragraph makes sense. Each word can only be used once.

| faster | gently | clear | sea | sparkles |

When it begins, the brook flows _____ through the vegetation. It

flows _____ the nearer it gets to the _____. The poet

describes how it appears to be _____ as it washes over pebbly

stones and _____ when the children are playing in it.

4 Explain in your own words what the lines 'Blossoms floating/Mimic boating' in verse four mean.

2

_____

_____

Find the **THREE**-letter word that is needed to complete each word from the text, so that each sentence makes sense. The missing three letters must make a word.

2

5 Children played on the _____ks of the brook.

6 The dappled sunshine and s_____e made the brook look pretty.

7 Which is closest in meaning to the word 'rippling' in verse two? Underline the correct answer from options **a–e**.

1

a making small waves

b gurgling slowly

c rushing violently

d making large splashes

e falling in a steady stream

8 This sentence has been jumbled up and has **ONE** extra word. Underline the word that is not needed.

1

sea eventually flows brook into the the mountain

Total 15

Read the text carefully and answer the questions that follow.

White Fang by Jack London
Extract from Chapter 1: The Trail of the Meat
Dark spruce forest frowned on either side the frozen waterway. The trees
had been stripped by a recent wind of their white covering of frost, and they
seemed to lean towards each other, black and ominous, in the fading light. A
vast silence reigned over the land. The land itself was a desolation, lifeless,
without movement, so lone and cold that the spirit of it was not even that   **5**
of sadness. There was a hint in it of laughter, but of a laughter more terrible
than any sadness—a laughter that was mirthless as the smile of the sphinx, a
laughter cold as the frost and partaking of the grimness of infallibility. It was the
masterful and incommunicable wisdom of eternity laughing at the futility of life
and the effort of life. It was the Wild, the savage, frozen-hearted Northland Wild.   **10**

But there *was* life, abroad in the land and defiant. Down the frozen waterway
toiled a string of wolfish dogs. Their bristly fur was rimed with frost. Their
breath froze in the air as it left their mouths, spouting forth in spumes of
vapour that settled upon the hair of their bodies and formed into crystals of
frost. Leather harness was on the dogs, and leather traces attached them to a   **15**
sled which dragged along behind. The sled was without runners. It was made
of stout birch-bark, and its full surface rested on the snow. The front end of
the sled was turned up, like a scroll, in order to force down and under the bore
of soft snow that surged like a wave before it. On the sled, securely lashed,
was a long and narrow oblong box. There were other things on the sled—   **20**
blankets, an axe, and a coffee-pot and frying-pan; but prominent, occupying
most of the space, was the long and narrow oblong box.

1   Where do the events in the passage take place? Underline one of options **a–e**
to answer the question.

   a on an icy lake

   b in a small wooden hut

   c down a frozen waterway through a forest

   d in a dense forest of birch trees

   e on an icy road

2 Choose and underline **TWO** phrases from options **a–e** that could correctly complete the sentence.

In the opening paragraph, which describes the setting of the story, we learn that:

a there was no sound

b laughter could be heard

c the trees were white with frost

d it was getting dark

e the trees stood straight

Select the **ONE** word on the right that has the most **SIMILAR** meaning to the word on the left, taken from the text. Underline the correct answer.

3 ominous   **a** spindly   **b** sinister   **c** powerful   **d** cold   **e** bare

4 futility   **a** fragility   **b** strength   **c** resilience   **d** effort   **e** pointlessness

Select the **TWO** odd words out on each line. Select your answers by underlining **TWO** of the options **a–e**.

5   **a** desolation   **b** bleakness   **c** laughter   **d** lifelessness   **e** movement

6   **a** worked   **b** lived   **c** laboured   **d** toiled   **e** settled

7 Find **TWO** ways in the second paragraph that the author shows the effect of the weather on the dogs.

> **FINDING CLUES**
> Look closely at the description of the dogs. How can you tell it is cold? Look for clues about their appearance or behaviour. Make sure you find TWO different things.

_____

_____

8 How were the dogs joined to the sled?

_____

9 Describe the item that took up the most room on the sled.

_____

Total   10

Test 16

Read the text carefully and answer the questions that follow.

The Real Princess by Hans Christian Andersen

There was once a prince who wished to marry a princess; but then she must be a real princess. He travelled all over the world in hopes of finding such a lady; but there was always something wrong. Princesses he found in plenty; but whether they were real princesses it was impossible for him to decide, for now one thing, now another, seemed to him not quite right about the ladies. At last, he returned to his palace quite cast down, because he wished so much to have a real princess for his wife.

5

One evening a fearful tempest arose, it thundered and lightened, and the rain poured down from the sky in torrents: besides, it was as dark as pitch. All at once there was heard a violent knocking at the door, and the old king, the prince's father, went out himself to open it.

10

It was a princess who was standing outside the door. What with the rain and the wind, she was in a sad condition; the water trickled down from her hair, and her clothes clung to her body. She said she was a real princess.

"Ah! we shall soon see about that!" thought the old queen-mother; however, she said not a word of what she was going to do; but went quietly into the bedroom, took all the bedclothes off the bed, and put three little peas on the bedstead. She then laid twenty mattresses one upon another over the three peas, and put twenty feather beds over the mattresses.

15

Upon this bed the princess was to pass the night.

20

The next morning, she was asked how she had slept. "Oh, very badly indeed!" she replied. "I have scarcely closed my eyes the whole night through. I do not know what was in my bed, but I had something hard under me, and am all over black and blue. It has hurt me so much!"

Now it was plain that the lady must be a real princess, since she had been able to feel the three little peas through the twenty mattresses and twenty feather beds. None but a real princess could have had such a delicate sense of feeling.

25

The prince accordingly made her his wife; being now convinced that he had found a real princess. The three peas were however put into the cabinet of curiosities, where they are still to be seen, provided they are not lost.

30

Wasn't this a lady of real delicacy?

READING CAREFULLY

This story is a fairy tale, told in a traditional style. Sometimes the order of words is a little different to modern retellings and the punctuation may be used differently, especially the semi-colon. Try to read through the whole sentence to get the flow and understand the meaning.

1 Underline the **TWO** answers that could **NOT** complete the sentence correctly from options **a–e**.

The prince had searched all over the world:

a but returned to his palace without a bride

b for a real princess to marry

c but found no princesses on his travels

d but had doubts about whether the ladies he met were real princesses

e found it easy to decide if the ladies he met were real princesses

2 Underline the correct answer from options **a–e**.

In line 6, the phrase 'quite cast down' means that the prince:

a had been turned down

b was feeling despondent

c was unsure about the princesses

d did not wish to marry

e did not like the palace

Select the **TWO** odd words out on each line. Select your answers by underlining **TWO** of the options **a–e**.

3   **a** tempest   **b** storm   **c** raining   **d** gale   **e** sunny

4   **a** convinced   **b** thoughtful   **c** sure   **d** possible   **e** certain

5 Find **TWO** ways in the third paragraph that the author shows the effect of the weather on the princess at the door.

_____

_____

6 This sentence has been jumbled up and has **ONE** extra word. Underline the word that is not needed.

queen-mother a she real princess felt because the knew was she the peas mattress

7 What happened to the peas eventually, according to the story?

_____

Total   8

Test 17

Read the text carefully and answer the questions that follow.

Hobbies on a Budget

Time to spare? Looking for a new pastime? Fed up with spending lots of money on leisure activities? Look no further than our great list of hobbies that will keep you occupied and not cost a fortune.

Start a blog

Choose a topic you feel passionate about and set up your own blog to share
your ideas. If you love films, TV or theatre, you could review productions you
have watched. Sports lovers could write about their own sporting interests or
events they have attended. Avid readers could discuss their thoughts about
their latest literary finds. The list is endless – just remember to keep your
identity, and that of others, private. Setting up a blog is quite straightforward
and there are many hosting sites that allow you to do so free of charge.

Photography

Taking interesting photographs with your phone is easier than ever.
Photographing ordinary objects or places from unusual perspectives can give
your photographs more appeal. Using filters to alter the colouring or style
of the finished image is also quite easy to do and can add an extra sense of
intrigue to your photographs. You can even use your photos to tell a story or
make a point about an issue, such as pollution.

Learn to juggle …

… Or braid hair, or draw a dog or whatever new skill takes your fancy. The
Internet is full of experts sharing their skills for others to learn, via short video
tutorials. Choose a skill you have always wanted to master, and get practising.
To ensure your new hobby remains economical, choose something that needs
minimal equipment.

Upcycling

Upcycling is the reuse of discarded everyday objects, such as clothes, in
creative ways, to produce exciting new items. For example, an old pair of
jeans can be turned into a bag, an old sweatshirt can be turned into a dog
bed, or a jam jar can be turned into a candle holder. Not only is this a low-
budget hobby, but it is environmentally friendly and can improve your craft
skills too. The only limit is your own imagination.

Board-games party

Most people have a board game or two gathering dust somewhere. Invite your
friends or family to a board-game party. Select two or three games that do not
take too long to play and allocate points to the winner for each game. At the
end of the night, add up who has won most and award them a silly prize!

5

10

15

20

25

30

35

1 Give **THREE** reasons why you might want to take up one of the hobbies suggested in the article.

3

_____

_____

_____

Select the **ONE** word on the right that has the most **SIMILAR** meaning to the word on the left. Underline the correct answer.

3

2 avid   **a** fast   **b** keen   **c** good   **d** regular   **e** slow

3 intrigue   **a** colour   **b** style   **c** perspective   **d** fascination   **e** space

4 economical   **a** quick   **b** special   **c** valuable   **d** worthwhile   **e** inexpensive

5 Give **TWO** additional benefits of trying upcycling as a hobby, apart from it being cheap to do.

2

_____

_____

6 Which of the following is **NOT** a hobby suggested in the article? Underline the correct answer from options **a–e**.

1

a making new products from unwanted items

b writing about one of your interests

c learning to braid hair

d cooking for a party

e telling a story using images

7 Find the missing **THREE** letters that complete these words. The three letters must make a word. The same three letters are used for both words.

1

COM __ __ __ ITION   AP __ __ __ ISING

Total   10

Test 18

Read the text carefully and answer the questions that follow.

The Months by Christina Rossetti
January cold desolate;
February all dripping wet;
March wind ranges;
April changes;
Birds sing in tune   5
To flowers of May,
And sunny June
Brings longest day;
In scorched July
The storm-clouds fly   10
Lightning-torn;
August bears corn,
September fruit;
In rough October
Earth must disrobe her;   15
Stars fall and shoot
In keen November;
And night is long
And cold is strong
In bleak December.   20

READING POETRY
Read the poem through a couple of times if it is short like this one. Try to 'hear' the words in your head and look out for rhythm and rhyme.

1 According to the poet, in which months would the weather be cold?   ☐ 1

_____

2 According to the poet, in which month would the birds sing?   ☐ 1

_____

3 According to the poet, in which month are you likely to see a stormy sky?   ☐ 1

_____

Test continues after Answers section →

ANSWERS

Test 1

(pages 4–5)

1 d all of the above.

Line 2 refers to 'limited food supplies' and states that they should be 'fairly distributed'. Lines 3–4 state that the government intended to ensure people had a 'nutritious, although not always exciting, diet to maintain the nation's health'.

2 In lines 6–7, the text refers to poorer people benefiting because they could now access nutritious food, which they may not have been able to afford before. This was because rationed foods were now available at a standard price to everyone, and everyone had the same rations.

3 c better health.

Lines 8–9 state that 'the health of the general public actually improved'. This showed that not only could poor people now afford healthier food, but also the rations allowed everyone equal access to a balanced diet.

4 b extra.

The text states that this was to cater for their extra nutritional needs, meaning that pregnant women and children needed extra vitamins and minerals, and manual workers used more energy, so they were entitled to extra rations.

5 The words 'valuable' (1 mark) and 'integral' (1 mark) in line 16 show that growing your own vegetables was considered important, since 'valuable' means worth a lot and 'integral' means a central part of something.

6 e some of the above.

'advice' and 'suggesting' (line 18) show that the Ministry of Food was an advisory body and did not make strict rules that the public had to follow.

7 'simple' suggests the recipe is not difficult for people to follow (1 mark). 'economical' suggests the recipe will not cost too much money (1 mark). Both points must be explained for 2 marks.

8 'substituting' means replacing one thing with another (see line 23 where the word 'replace' is used). An answer might refer to some expensive or scarce foods being replaced by others, as mentioned in the text. Any answer that refers to the use of one food in place of another is acceptable.

9 1 mark each for any two of the following from lines 23–27:

carrots or parsnips replacing sugar;

powdered eggs being used instead of fresh eggs;

the use of mashed potato in biscuits;

pig's offal replacing goose.

Test 2

(pages 6–7)

1 The months appear to be 'playing a game' because they seem to have swapped temperatures. The summer was cool, when it should have been hot, but September was unbearably hot, not cool as autumn should be. The text suggests the months have a personality 'as if September were determined to show that he knew how to make himself just as disagreeable as August'. We call this 'personification'.

2 b humid and oppressive.

The word 'sultry' means that it is a humid sort of heat, with warm, moist air, suggesting it is oppressive. The efforts of the children to help Cousin Helen stay cool also reinforce the idea that it is uncomfortable.

3 a providing shade (1 mark);

c making sure she had cold drinks (1 mark);

d taking her outside in the evening (1 mark).

'sitting on the sofa with her' is not mentioned (just wheeling the sofa), so this should NOT be ticked. The number of marks allocated to the question gives a clue to how many boxes should be ticked.

4 d withered leaves.

The leaves are 'wrinkled' (line 11), which is closest in meaning to 'withered'. This is reinforced by the description of the hot weather.

The correct answer can also be arrived at by elimination: leaves are specifically mentioned, so 'no leaves' can be ruled out. There is no mention of their size, so 'small leaves' can be eliminated. 'green leaves' can also be eliminated because they are described as being of an 'ugly colour' rather than any particular colour.

5 Dust.

This answer can be found in the phrase 'the yellow dust hanging in the air' (line 10).

6 'trying' (see line 13) suggests that everyone's patience was tested during September. 'disagreeable' (line 4) indicates what the weather was like, but not necessarily that it tested everyone's patience.

7 'furnace' (line 15).

If the word 'furnace' is not known, it can be deduced from the context, as the sentence mentions the wind being 'burned' (last line).

8 True: a In October, the weather stayed hot. See lines 13–14: 'made little difference'; **d** There was no improvement in the dusty atmosphere in October. See line 14: 'still the dust continued'.

False: b In October, there was a refreshing breeze. Lines 14–15 mention the wind (of which 'breeze' is a synonym) seeming to be heated by a furnace and says that it brought no refreshment; **c** October was a very windy month. See line 14: 'when it blew' implies that it did not blow often.

9 a boiled red like lobsters – simile: the leaves are compared to the colour of lobsters (1 mark);

b he knew how to make himself just as disagreeable as August – personification: September is described as if it were a person (1 mark);

c excessively sultry – description: a description of the weather (1 mark)

Test 3

(pages 8–9)

1 excited: shown by the words 'I can't wait to see …' (1 mark); incredulous: shown by the words 'I can't believe …' (1 mark). Answers can include 'Brazil at last' to show either excitement or incredulity.

2 'vast', in the first line, is a synonym for big and means particularly wide or expansive.

3 a people and buildings.

This can be deduced from the use of the word 'civilisation' (line 12), which means an area that has been developed by humans.

4 a 'plant life' is the closest in meaning to vegetation.

'treetops' and 'vegetables' are too specific, and 'plant-eating' is not a noun, but an adjective.

5 True: a there was a space with no trees. See line 16: 'a flat clearing' (1 mark);

d there was plenty of wood around. See line 18: 'many fallen branches all around' (1 mark).

False: b and **c** are false as the text says the clearing was close to the river and that it was flat (line 16), so not on a slope.

6 Answers may refer to the following for a maximum of three marks:

He keeps her safe, as he knows where the insects are and which fruit to eat (1 mark);

He shows her how to do things, such as build a shelter and fish using a wooden spear (1 mark);

He tells her what wildlife to look out for, such as the pink dolphins (1 mark).

7 Facts: b Not all forest fruits are safe to eat – this is fact as it states that Carlito shows her which fruits *are* safe to eat (lines 25–26);

c Some insect bites can kill you – this is fact as Jen states that 'one sting or bite from some of these tiny insects can … even prove fatal', meaning it can kill you (lines 28–30).

Opinions: a Woolly monkeys are funny – this is Jen's opinion as she watches them play (line 20);

d Pink dolphins are beautiful to look at – this is Jen's opinion when she says 'What a sight!' (lines 14–15).

Test 4

(pages 10–11)

1 **b** 'darted about'.

'Dart' as a verb means to move suddenly or rapidly. This is closest in meaning to the verb 'flit', which means to move swiftly and lightly.

2 **True: b** On winter evenings, the only light comes from the fire. See line 6: 'fire gave the only light';

c Iceland is a long way north. See line 1: 'far north'.

False: a It is never warm in Iceland. Line 3 mentions 'the warm season';

d It took lots of concentration to spin, weave and knit. See lines 9–10: 'The work left their minds free to think and their lips to talk', which implies that it did not take much concentration so they were free to think and talk about other things.

3 **True: c** They wanted them to find out more about some Norwegian legends. See lines 13–14: it says that they wanted them to love 'old Norway' (1 mark);

d They wanted to inspire them to be courageous. See the question posed by the fathers in line 13: 'What will make them brave and wise?' 'Courageous' is a synonym for 'brave' (1 mark).

NOT TRUE: The following three are not true because:

a They wanted them to learn how to hunt – this is not mentioned in relation to the tales.

b They knew the children had already learnt about their heroes – in lines 12–13 it states that the fathers were worried about their children 'not learning much'.

e They wanted them to stop sitting by the fire – the text says that a 'whole family would sit ... around the fire'. The text does not suggest that the fathers wanted to stop the children sitting by the fire.

4 **a** 'voyages' in line 17 is a word for a long sea journey (1 mark);

b 'recording' in line 25 is another word for writing down (1 mark);

c 'harp' in line 19 is the instrument played by the men who sang the skalds (1 mark).

5 At first, the sagas were passed on by hearing them sung, rather than written down, because 'few people wrote or read' (lines 21–22).

6 The Icelandic people were too busy in the warmer weather to tell tales. Lines 2–4 of the text say: 'During the warm season, they used to fish, produce fish oil, hunt seabirds, gather feathers, tend their sheep and make hay.'

7 Icelanders used their sheep for wool (answers may make references from the first paragraph to spinning, weaving and knitting their wool for 1 mark); and for vellum (answers may make reference to the final paragraph to making pages for books for 1 mark).

Test 5

(pages 12–13)

1 Travelling along one day, a young man **noticed** a **purse** at the **side** of the road. He **gloated** about finding it and refused to **split** the **cash** with his **companion**. When an angry **throng** pursued him, however, his fellow traveller got his own back.

2 **d** apart ('near', 'close' and 'beside' are all synonyms for 'together'; 'often' is an adverb of time)

3 **e** luck ('misfortune' means bad luck)

4 **b** whisper ('shout' is a loud vocal noise and 'whisper' is the quietest vocal noise listed, so is therefore the best answer)

5 **c** thought it was unfair to expect the money to be shared.
The use of the word 'indignantly' implies that he thought it was unfair. Being indignant means that someone is showing anger or annoyance about what they think is unfair treatment.

6 An acceptable answer will refer to the context – an angry crowd approaching and calling him thief – as a clue that the man thinks they are in trouble and may get hurt or beaten if they are caught with the purse.

A literal response – i.e. saying that they will get lost – is not acceptable for a mark.

7 The word 'approaching' tells the reader that the crowd is getting closer to the travellers.

Answers may also suggest it implies they know who the thieves are.

8 PAN: PANIC, COMPANION

9 'I' shows how the first man does not want to share the money. Later, the second man uses it to show he does not want to share the blame (1 mark).

'We' shows that the second man thinks the money should be shared. Later, the first man uses it because he wants to share the blame (1 mark). Italics are used to emphasise the words.

Test 6

(pages 14–15)

1 1912 – 'maiden voyage' in the first sentence means *Titanic's* first voyage.

2 'fateful' and 'disaster' both indicate that something bad happened to *Titanic*. Both must be given for a mark.

3 **True: d** Violet Jessop survived two shipping disasters. The second bullet point refers to the fact that she survived the sinking of *Britannic* too;

e More lifeboats were required after the disaster. The fifth bullet point refers to regulations to improve safety on ships after the *Titanic* disaster, including the requirement for more lifeboats.

False: a *Titanic* was the only ship of its kind at the time. The first bullet point states that it had a sister ship called *Olympic*;

b There were no survivors when *Titanic* sank. The second second and third bullet points say that Violet Jessop and two dogs survived;

c Letters waiting to be sent by passengers were saved. The fourth bullet point refers to the sacks of mail, which would include letters, as being lost when the ship sank.

4 **Historically valuable:** The menus are historically valuable because they tell us more about life on board, how different classes were treated and some specific details about the food eaten on the voyage. Answers should refer to one or more of these aspects (1 mark).

Financially valuable: The menus are financially valuable because they are worth lots of money, as shown by the price of £58 000 when one was sold at auction (1 mark).

5 **d** the food in first class was as good as the best restaurants in France – as suggested by the word 'rivalled'.

Options **a** and **c** are both incorrect as there is no evidence that either all the food or chefs were French, although they may have been. Option **b** is also incorrect as the term 'rivalled' suggests a comparison rather than their being literally in competition.

6 insight

7 eerie

8 investigate

9 submersible

Test 7

(pages 16–17)

1 **b** the majority of peppered moths were pale with black speckles (1 mark);

c a few peppered moths were darker (1 mark).

Note that the number of marks allocated to the question gives a clue to how many boxes should be ticked. If one is missing or one extra statement is marked true, only award one mark. If all are marked true, do not award any marks.

2 'vast' means large (amounts).

3 During the Industrial Revolution, many **factories** were built, containing newly invented **machinery**. Unfortunately, these often caused **pollution**, which resulted in trees becoming **coated** in a layer of **soot**. The change in surroundings meant that lighter-coloured moths were more **noticeable**, which made them easy **prey**. The darker moths became more **prevalent**.

4 The reduction in pollution is due to the introduction of new laws about air quality (lines 18–19).

5 b 'assessed' is the closest in meaning to 'calculated' in this context (line 15) as the use of a percentage later in the sentence suggests it is more precise than a prediction or observation.

6 b 'mainly' is closest in meaning to 'predominantly' in this context (line 3) where it refers to the overall colour of each moth.

Test 8

(pages 18–19)

1 They defined silence as the absence of sound or no sound.

2 b He enjoyed being inventive with his music. This statement best sums up John Cage's approach, which the text describes as 'pushing the boundaries', and his liking to 'experiment' in lines 7–8.

Both **a** and **c** are incorrect because although he used these two elements (silence and electronic instruments), the text shows he does not use them exclusively. He studied with renowned composers (lines 6–7) so **d** is incorrect, as is **e**, because he welcomed the environmental sounds in his piece *4'33"* (lines 18–19).

3 Inverted commas are used in line 18 to show that there may not actually be a 'piece' of music as most people would define it.

4 e 'duration' is closest in meaning to 'time'.

5 a 'renowned' is closest in meaning to 'acclaimed'.

6 Cage was born in America.

'composed' is not needed.

7 The performers do not play their instruments in the piece. OR In the piece, the performers do not play their instruments.

'sounds' is not needed.

Note that although 'sounds' would make sense in place of 'instruments', reference to this particular text would show 'instruments' as the best answer: 'the score directs the performers not to play their instruments' (lines 16–17).

8 d performance.

The text states (lines 19–20) that the piece will 'change every time it is performed'.

9 b unusual.

The text states that the performers are given directions that they should 'not play their instruments', which is not usual.

The text states that this instruction is given so option **c** 'no' is incorrect. It is also clear rather than vague, so option **a** is incorrect. It is not complicated and there are not many instructions, so options **d** and **e** are incorrect.

Test 9

(pages 20–21)

1 The word 'misfortune' (meaning bad luck) implies the visit did not go well.

2 Complaint 1: the long wait. See line 4: 'not only were we left waiting' (1 mark);

Complaint 2: they had lost the booking. See line 6: 'could find no record' (1 mark).

3 d 'examined' is closest to 'perused' as it suggests a longer look rather than just a 'glance'.

4 The range of food available ~~was~~/was not extensive because it says that only 'two of the five starters' were available and there were no new potatoes, only chips (lines 10–11).

To gain the mark, both the correct word ('was') should be crossed out and at least one of these two reasons included in the answer.

5 unappealing, cold, congealed, soft, grey, raw (1 mark each for any **two** of these).

The instructions specifically ask for adjectives to be given, not descriptive phrases, so 'the appearance of worn leather' should not be awarded a mark.

6 The desserts were **better** than the main course, although the experience was spoilt by the service being **slow**. When Coral Jones paid the bill, she told the **staff** that she was **disappointed**, but their response was **impolite**.

7 **b** say sorry; **d** offer compensation; **e** train the staff. (All three need to be underlined for 1 mark.)

Coral asks for the written reply herself ('I look forward to your written reply' on line 26) and she asks for compensation, but does not ask for an invitation for a return visit.

Test 10

(pages 22–23)

1 **b** not used by ordinary people.

It can be inferred that they were not usually used by ordinary people from lines 5–6: 'were a sign of privilege and were only used by the rich and powerful'.

This also shows umbrellas were not an 'everyday item', so **d** is incorrect. Answer **a** is incorrect: being used by women refers to umbrellas in Europe (lines 12–13), therefore not the earliest umbrellas. There is no mention of them being specifically religious, so **c** is incorrect. The Chinese used wax, but these were not 'the earliest umbrellas' as specified in the question, so **e** is incorrect.

2 **Design:** The Chinese improved umbrellas by covering the paper shades in wax, which made them waterproof (1 mark).

Usefulness: This meant that they could be used to keep people dry in the rain (1 mark).

3 Historians know about ancient Egyptian umbrellas from the pictures and carvings of them in Egyptian ruins.

4 **c** 'mainly', which means 'for the most part' and not any of other options given.

5 **d** 'outdated'

c 'old' is close as an antonym (opposite) of 'fashionable', but isn't as accurate as 'outdated' in terms of fashion.

6 Nowadays, a wide range of umbrellas can be easily **purchased** for an **affordable** price. Although the **design** is still similar to the earliest umbrellas, new innovations have included various additions to the **handle** and space to see out of the **hood**.

'expensive' and 'invented' should be the words not used.

Test 11

(pages 24–25)

1 **e** he had been given it.

This is the best answer because line 3 states that the butcher had 'thrown a bone'.

There is no clear suggestion that the dog begged, so **c** is not the best answer. **a** is incorrect because he did not 'win a prize' – 'prize' in the context of line 3 refers to how the dog felt about his treasured bone. It is true that he was in a hurry (**d**), but this did not cause him to have the bone, and the text refers to his foolishness, so he is not clever (**b**).

2 **c** wide

'big' (**d**) is the closest possible other opposite, but does not imply the closer relationship to the concept of dimension that 'wide' does.

3 The dog saw his own **reflection** in the river, but was **confused**. Thinking he had seen **another** dog, he was **jealous** of the dog's **larger** bone. He **jumped** into the water but, in doing so, lost his **own** bone.

'special', 'mirror' and 'stray' should be the words not used.

4 'swimming for dear life' means the dog had to keep swimming in order to stay alive and get to the shore/not drown.

5 The foolish dog jumped into the water.

'bone' is not needed.

6 **d** it was difficult to climb out of the water.

Although all of answers **a–c** may be true, they do not explain the words in the line quoted.

7 **a** a greedy dog who wanted more.

This is shown by lines 6–9 of the text, which describe him as 'greedy' and wanting the bone of the other dog.

d a covetous dog who learnt his lesson. Lines 15–16 of the text imply that he learnt his lesson and 'covetous' refers to him being jealous of the bone.

Test 12

(pages 26–27)

1 b to show the shape of some islands more clearly.

This is the best answer because line 3 states that the photography 'revealed the unusual shape of many islands'.

There is no suggestion that the islands were not discovered before (**a**), just that their shape was now more easily seen. The other three options all use words from the text ('birds', 'space', 'objects'), but these are not things that are being photographed according to the text.

2 e is in a volcanic area.

This is shown by lines 8–9: 'one of the most volcanically active places in the world'.

The text states it was formed from six volcanoes (not a single one), so option **a** is incorrect. It is one of the Galapagos Islands rather than near them, so option **b** is incorrect, and the text does not say how many there are, so **c** is also incorrect. The text states it is off the 'northwestern coast of South America' so therefore **d** is incorrect as it is 'off the coast', not on the mainland.

3 d 'flourish' is the closest synonym for 'thrive'. Although 'reproduce' (**c**) may be considered, this is more specific and 'flourish' is the better option.

4 c 'located' is the closest synonym for 'situated'. 'put' can mean 'situated', but not in the context used here.

5 e 'barren' is the opposite of 'lush' when used in the context of describing landscapes (rather than population, which 'uninhabited' implies). Options **b–d** are synonyms.

6 d 'natural' is the opposite of 'man-made' when describing landscape features, as in the text.

7 a 'populated' is the opposite of 'uninhabited', not to be confused with 'popular'.

None of the others are a clear opposite, even if they may be used in connection with being populated.

8 CAN: UNCANNILY, VOLCANIC

9 OIL: UNSPOILT, SOIL

10 1 mark each for any four of the following:

the beauty – 'what could be more beautiful' (line 19);

coral-reef, dolphin-shaped island off its coast (lines 19-20);

'unspoilt villages' (line 22);

'lush forests' (line 22);

'picture-perfect beaches' (line 22);

'smouldering volcanoes' (line 23);

seeing Komodo dragons (line 24).

Test 13

(pages 28–29)

1 e fabled creatures found in myths from Scandinavia.

As stated in line 2, they are mythical creatures in Scandinavian folklore. 'fabled' is another word for 'mythical'.

2 1 mark each for any five of the following, either directly quoted or in the child's own words: ugly face/grotesque brutish features; either dwarf or giant (small or large also acceptable); long prominent noses; hairy/long wild hair; sharp teeth or tusks.

The words 'rude' and 'aggressive' are not correct, as the question asks about appearance.

3 Trolls live in dark caves or the craggy rocks in mountains (lines 14-15). 'Castles' would not be acceptable because they only appear in 'some' stories, not 'most'.

4 b their name, in the old Norse language, reflects their behaviour towards humans.

See the penultimate paragraph, which states that their name means 'evil' in ancient Norse and that they try to harm humans.

The other options are incorrect because their appearance and where they live is not relevant to the name (options **a** and **d**), sending nasty messages is the modern meaning of 'troll' (option **c**) and their name does not mean 'dwarf' (option **e**).

5 c grumble; **e** outsmart

The others are all related in meaning to 'threaten'.

6 **b** famous; **d** ugly

The others all mean 'likely to attack or confront'.

7 'The troll was no match for the final billy goat' means that the troll was not strong enough to overpower the final billy goat/the final billy goat was stronger.

Test 14

(pages 30–31)

1 The brook starts 'from a fountain in a mountain' (lines 1 and 2).

2 'from', 'in' and 'through' are the three prepositions found in verse one.

3 When it begins, the brook flows **gently** through the vegetation. It flows **faster** the nearer it gets to the **sea**. The poet describes how it appears to be **clear** as it washes over pebbly stones and **sparkles** when the children are playing in it.

4 'Blossoms floating/Mimic boating' means that blossoms (or flowers) have fallen into the water of the brook (1 mark) and are floating along, imitating the movement of boats (1 mark).

Both parts must be explained for 2 marks.

5 ban: banks

6 had: shade

7 **a** making small waves.

This is closest in meaning to 'rippling' as it describes the physical effect, rather than the sound.

'rippling' implies a more gentle effect of water flowing than suggested in options **c–e**. Option **b** ('gurgles slowly') is not correct as the verse implies the brook flows quickly (e.g. 'darted', 'hurrying').

8 The brook eventually flows into the sea.

'mountain' is not needed.

Test 15

(pages 32–33)

1 **c** down a frozen waterway through a forest.

Option **a** is incorrect as line 1 of the text says 'a waterway' rather than a body of water like a

lake. No wooden huts or roads are mentioned so options **b** and **e** are incorrect. **d** is incorrect as line 1 of the text states it is a 'spruce forest'.

2 **a** there was no sound. See lines 3–4: 'a vast silence reigned over the land';

d it was getting dark. See line 3: 'in the fading light' implies it was getting dark.

Both must be identified for the mark.

3 **b** sinister.

'ominous' means threatening or menacing, so none of the other options have a similar meaning.

4 **e** pointlessness.

'futility' means ineffectiveness or uselessness, so none of the other options have a similar meaning.

5 **c** laughter; **e** movement

The others are all related in meaning to 'desolation'.

6 **b** lived; **e** settled

The others are all related in meaning to 'worked'.

7 1 mark each for any two of the following:

the fur bristling with frost (line 12);

their breath freezing in the air (line 13);

the vapour freezing into crystals on the dogs' fur (lines 14–15).

8 The dogs were attached to the sled with leather straps and a leather harness (lines 15–16).

9 The item that took up the most room on the sled was a long, narrow, oblong box (lines 21–22).

Test 16

(pages 34–35)

1 **c** but found no princesses on his travels. See line 3: 'Princesses he found in plenty';

e found it easy to decide if the ladies he met were real princesses. See line 4: 'whether they were real princesses it was impossible for him to decide'.

Both must be identified for the mark.

2 b was feeling despondent.

'cast down' and 'despondent' both mean discouraged and dejected.

3 c raining; **e** sunny

Not only are they not synonyms for 'tempest', but they are also adjectives, whereas the others are all nouns.

4 b thoughtful; **d** possible

The others are linked by being adjectives describing certainty.

5 She had water trickling from her hair (1 mark). Her clothes were wet and clung to her body (1 mark).

6 The queen-mother knew she was a real princess because she felt the peas.

'mattress' is not needed.

7 The peas were put on display in a cabinet of interesting things ('curiosities'), according to the story (lines 29–30).

Test 17

(pages 36–37)

1 All correct answers are found in the rhetorical questions of lines 1–2 of the text.

Reason 1: You have spare time (1 mark).

Reason 2: You are looking for something new to do ('a new pastime') (1 mark).

Reason 3: You are tired of spending lots of money on a hobby ('fed up with spending lots of money on leisure activities') (1 mark).

For the last reason, the answer must refer to more than being economical – it must specify this is in response to other hobbies having cost too much.

2 b keen

None of the other words has a similar meaning

3 d fascination

'intrigue' can mean 'something that fascinates'.

4 e inexpensive

Both 'economical' and 'inexpensive' can mean 'cheap' or 'low-budget'.

5 Upcycling is 'environmentally friendly' (1 mark) and it can improve your skills in craft (1 mark). See lines 30–31.

6 d cooking for a party.

The other options are paraphrases of the hobbies given in the article.

7 PET: COMPETITION, APPETISING

Test 18

(pages 38, 59)

1 January and December. See line 1: 'January cold desolate' and lines 20–21: 'And cold is strong/In bleak December'.

2 May. See lines 5–6: 'Birds sing in tune/To flowers of May'. Note the lack of punctuation at the end of line 5, meaning the birds' singing refers to the month of May, not a continuation of April, as there is a semi-colon.

3 July. See lines 9–10: 'In scorched July/The storm-clouds fly'.

4 June and December are opposites because of: the temperature – June is 'sunny', December is 'cold' and 'bleak' (1 mark);

the length of day – June 'Brings longest day' whereas in December 'night is long' (1 mark).

5 d burnt.

'scorch' means burn the surface of something with a flame or heat.

6 b a harsh month.

See line 14, which refers to October being 'rough'. 'rough' is a synonym for 'harsh'

7 b the leaves falling off the tress.

'Earth must disrobe her' refers to the leaves all falling from the trees.

8 The poem is about how each of the **months** of the year are **different**. In particular, the **weather** varies greatly. For example, in **February**, it often **rains** a lot according to the poem. By contrast, **June** is a very **warm** time of year. August and September are when crops are most **abundant**.

Test 19

(pages 60–61)

1 Tenrecs' poor eyesight is not a problem because they are nocturnal (see line 15), i.e. they come out after dark (1 mark) and 'rely heavily on their sense of smell and hearing' (see line 16) (1 mark).

2 **e** on Madagascar and in regions of mainland Africa.

   See lines 1–3, which state where they live – 'all over the island of Madagascar' and 'some parts of mainland Africa'.

3 **c** both plants and animals.

   See line 13, where the term 'omnivorous' is explained. Although lines 13–14 explain they largely eat invertebrates, the word 'largely' and the explanation of 'omnivorous' means this is not all they eat.

4 **d** 'defence' is closest in this context to 'protection' as in lines 20–21 the text describes the tenrec's spines as helping to keep it safe from predators.

5 There are many **species** of tenrec, although they all live either on the African **mainland** or the **island** of Madagascar, off the African coast. The largest tenrec is the **common** tenrec, and these weigh up to one kilogram. Birds and snakes are among the tenrecs' **predators**, but their **covering** of spines helps to **protect** them. Sadly, deforestation has destroyed much of their natural habitat and their **survival** is now under **threat**.

   'evolved' is the one word not used.

Test 20

(pages 62–63)

1 According to line 1 of the text, she wore green glasses – 'spectacles' is another word for glasses.

2 **e** green rain falling from the green sky.

   The sky is green according to line 7, but the author then describes the sun's rays, not rain (lines 7–8).

3 'the children all ran away' (1 mark) and 'hid behind their mothers' (1 mark) – line 12. This implies they were afraid of the Lion.

4 **c** the lack of animals.

   See line 18: 'There seemed to be no horses nor animals of any kind'. 'lack of' means without there being any of something.

5 **c** wealthy

   'prosperous' and 'wealthy' both mean 'to be well off financially'.

6 To enter the Palace, Dorothy and her **companions** had to **follow** the Guardian of the Gates. A soldier, whose **uniform** was green, allowed them to **enter**. The room they were led into was **furnished** in green too. They were asked to **wait** while the soldier took a message to the Throne Room.

Test 21

(pages 64–65)

1 **c** during the morning of a February day in 1947.

   This matches the statement in line 1 that states the date and time of day.

   None of the other options have the correct combination of place and/or time.

2 Five chores that can be included, taken from the first paragraph are:

   Farmers fed and watered their animals (livestock) (1 mark).

   Housewives tidied rooms and lit fires (1 mark).

   Miners went to work underground (1 mark).

   An artist started sketching (1 mark).

   A logging crew began logging (1 mark).

3 One example required in each section, from any of the following.

   Sights: 'large and brilliant fireball'; 'streaked across the sky' (and disappeared); 'large black column of smoke', 'tinged with a reddish-rose colour'; 'curved and then zigzag in form' (1 mark).

   Sounds: 'mighty thunderclap'; 'powerful roar like an artillery cannonade' (1 mark)

   Feelings: 'a strong airwave' (1 mark)

4 d He painted a picture straightaway before he could forget what he had seen.

See lines 31–32: he 'began a picture before his impressions of it could fade'.

Test 22

(pages 66–67)

1 d keeps on going, regardless of what is in his way.

See lines 2–4, where even running towards his favourite food does not cause him to stop.

Although Bertie is fast, this is not the meaning behind the simile given in the question.

2 'to our astonishment' (line 10) shows surprise on the part of the owners (1 mark);

'Thinking we had made a mistake' (line 11) shows they were so surprised that they made him do it again, in case they had got the timing wrong (1 mark).

3 d use of a special stopwatch.

The requirement to have two timekeepers is mentioned, but there is no reference to a stopwatch.

4 A possible answer to this open-response question might be:

Although the owners were worried on the morning of the attempt (line 21 refers to 'nerve-racking'), Bertie was unbothered (line 22) – 'unbothered is a synonym for 'unfazed' (1 mark).

Bertie was eager to perform – 'Bertie's legs were already sweeping the air' in lines 26–27; 'raring to go' in line 31 (1 mark).

5 a encouraged him.

This can be deduced from the words that follow in the text, which are the things that the onlookers shout to encourage Bertie.

Test 23

(pages 68–69)

1 e how places look at dawn.

See the first sentence: 'There is a time, between night and day (dawn), when landscapes (places) sleep.'

a is incorrect because, although we later read that Tom went to the garden doors at midnight (paragraph two), the question specifically refers to the opening paragraph. Options **b** and **c** are incorrect because the traveller is an example of someone who may have experienced how places look at dawn, and the long train journey cannot itself experience the landscape sleeping. The 'foggy morning' in option **d** is not referred to at all.

2 c was like a person who had kept watch.

A vigil is a period when someone deliberately stays awake to keep watch.

None of the other options accurately refer to this specific reference from the text, which uses personification to give the garden human characteristics and behaviours.

3 An owl.

The description of the bird comes first and then the kind of bird is given, after the use of a colon (line 17), to show this is the bird being referred to in the previous description.

4 1 mark each for any three of the following:

The bird seemed to fall from the fir tree (line 16 – 'seemed for a second to fall')

It made a sound (line 14 – 'One bird spoke')

It flew to a tree further away (lines 16–17 – 'was swept up and along, outspread, on a wind that never blew, to another, farther tree')

It looked dishevelled/as if it had been up all night (line 18 – 'ruffled, dazed appearance').

5 e nearest.

Although 'beside' might be thought to be a suitable option, it is a preposition, while 'nearest' and 'farthest' are opposite adjectives.

6 **c** dawn and **e** cloudy are not similar to 'gloom'. The word 'gloom' should be read in the sentence from lines 21–22 of the text: 'through the gloom of yew-trees arching overhead'. Both options must be identified to earn the mark.

Test 24

(pages 70–71)

1 **a** complicated rhythmic patterns (1 mark);

   c metal toe and heel plates (1 mark);

   d hitting the feet on the ground (1 mark).

   The intricate rhythms mentioned in **b** are not clapped but tapped with the feet (lines 2–3 state: 'By striking the floor with their feet in different ways, the dancer creates intricate and often very fast rhythms'). Drumming, in **e**, is mentioned in a later paragraph, but it is from this that tap dancing originated; it is not part of it.

2 The phrase 'seen on theatre stages the world over' means that tap dancing is now performed in shows (in theatres) all over the world.

   Both elements (performing and across the world) must be included to be awarded the mark.

3 **e** maintain a tradition.

   This refers to the desire to keep the custom or tradition of drumming alive in their new circumstances away from their homeland. Although several of the other options are linked to this, this one is the best answer because it directly paraphrases the given phrase.

4 Tap dancing **originated** in America, but it developed from the **tradition** of African drumming among slave **communities**. When their use of drums was **restricted**, they developed an **alternative** way of creating complex rhythms using the **feet**.

   'pattern' is the word not used.

5 **c** retreat; **e** panic

   The others are all similar in meaning, to do with resistance.

6 **b** variation; **e** dance

   The others are all similar in meaning, to do with traditions.

7 **c** amalgamation.

   This means a blend or mix of two or more things.

Test 25

(pages 72–73)

1 **c** taken scientists a long time to develop.

   See line 1: 'Years of research had gone into developing the seeds'. The other options only contain part of the information or are wrongly understood.

2 Answers should refer to two aspects of the phrase 'tiny pockets of life' (line 5): the size (very small) (1 mark) and the potential to grow into a useful crop (1 mark).

   Both should be referred to for two marks.

3 **c** a food that is eaten regularly and forms the major part of people's diets.

   The key word here to selecting the correct option is the adjective 'staple', which means 'main' or 'important'.

4 It will provide a staple food for millions of people (line 7) (1 mark).

   It can be fermented to provide a fuel (line 8) (1 mark).

   It grows very fast (line 9) (1 mark).

5 **d** everyone was nervous and excited.

   See line 14: 'Tension mixed with anticipation filled the air'. This is the closest explanation of the expression 'the whole lab seemed to hold its breath'.

6 **a** was like an arm or leg.

   'limb' in this context means 'arm or leg'.

7 **e** restrained.

   'Unleashed' means letting go of something by untying it or unrestricting it. 'Restrained' is when something is tied up or restricted.

Test 26

(pages 74–75)

1 b ice wears away the rock.

See lines 4–5: 'When **glaciers** develop they gradually move, eroding the rock beneath to carve away deep troughs', plus the information from the glossary explaining that it is a dense mass of compacted ice.

2 c gully.

This meaning can be inferred from the description of how the 'trough' is 'carved', in line 5, and also the following information on the same line, which further explains how this is a 'steep-sided U-shaped valley'.

3 e derives.

'derives' is the only word that means the same as 'originates' (line 12) and its meaning can be inferred from line 13, where the translation of the ancient Norse word is given as 'water body'.

The alternative options **a**, **b** and **d** are all verbs, but not direct synonyms, and option **c**, 'language', is connected to the topic but is a noun, not a verb.

4 The three natural features can be located in the paragraph entitled 'What is a fjord like?' Award 1 mark each for any three of the following:

'A deep, calm body of water' (line 15)

'dramatic, rugged mountains' (line 15)

'Huge waterfalls' (lines 16–17)

'islands' (line 18);

'rocky outcrops' (line 18).

Paraphrasing of these is acceptable, but there must be no man-made features included.

5 d unlike anything else.

Although all of the other options may be applicable to the fjord, they are not the same in meaning to 'unique'.

6 'influx' (line 28) means the arrival of a large number of people. See lines 26–27, which explain how the town caters for the arrival of the tourists during the spring and summer months.

7 In spring and summer, it is easier to get to Geirangerfjord. This is because the bitter cold weather in winter means that people cannot get there by land or sea.

Test 27

(pages 76–77)

1 b argumentative.

'quarrelsome' appears in the first paragraph (line 3), and describes the magpie.

While some of the other options may also apply to the description of the magpie in this paragraph, none of the other options have the same meaning as 'quarrelsome'.

2 c cleverly.

'cunningly' appears in the first paragraph (line 7) and refers to how the magpie builds its nest to keep out robbers. This is clever, rather than devious, so is the best choice from the given adverbs.

3 d a soldier in a red uniform.

See lines 13–14: 'his red body and long legs give him quite a military appearance – like a soldier at attention'.

a is incorrect because the reference is not to a soldier in battle, but to a soldier in uniform.

4 The vulture 'tidies up' by eating any dead animals (except their bones) that are left lying anywhere. This could be seen as helping out nature, as it is implied that the bodies do not have time to rot.

5 e He can swoop down quickly to catch his prey.

See lines 29–30: 'he swoops down on his prey like a thunderbolt from the sky ...'.

6 Although the **vulture** may be considered **helpful**, eating **dead** animals is not very **pleasant**. The **magpie** is not well liked either: other birds do not like him because he **steals** their eggs and farmers do not like him because of the damage he **causes**. Perhaps the most likeable bird in the text is the **flamingo**, owing to its attractive **colour**.

'enter', 'companions' and 'follow' are not used.

Test 28

(pages 78–79)

1 STING: DISTINGUISH

2 SPARE: TRANSPARENT

3 QUEST: UNQUESTIONABLY

4 **a** he could see bright light shining through the window. See lines 1–2, where it says it was dark and he could barely distinguish the window; **d** he saw a ferret running across his chamber. The reference to a ferret in the text (line 3) is a description of his eyes, not an actual animal.

Both these options must be selected for 1 mark.

5 **c** wrong.

'wrong' is the only word that is not a synonym for 'preposterous'.

6 **b** had to cling onto things to find where he was going in the dark.

The word 'grope' means to feel around blindly with hands, and the context of the piece shows that this was because it was so dark. The description of the darkness and Scrooge's response to it, in paragraph one, supports this.

7 Answers should refer to two aspects of Scrooge's behaviour:

He rubs the window with his dressing-gown sleeve to clear the frost – lines 16–17: 'was obliged to rub the frost off with the sleeve of his dressing-gown' (1 mark).

He looks out of the window to see what is happening in the street below – line 17 to the end of the paragraph (1 mark).

8 'and thought, and thought, and thought' (line 22) tells the reader that Scrooge was thinking for a long time, was confused and finding it difficult to work out what was happening. This can be deduced from the lines that follow (lines 23–24): 'the more he thought, the more perplexed he was'.

9 **c** ownership.

This can be deduced from the context of the word in line 21, where he describes how people had not 'taken possession of the day'.

Test 29

(pages 80–81)

1 **c** enemies

Bruce was fighting 'against his foes', which means they were enemies.

2 **b** the English king was trying to take power in Scotland.

See lines 3–4: 'The King of England was at war with him, and had led a great army into Scotland to drive him out of the land'.

This sentence also confirms that options **a**, **d** and **e** are incorrect. Lines 5–6 ('led his brave little army') show that **c** is wrong.

3 When Bruce was in hiding, he was feeling exhausted (1 mark) and ready to give up/felt defeated (1 mark). See lines 10–11: 'he was tired and sick at heart, and ready to give up all hope'.

4 The spider inspires Bruce because she attempts something difficult six times and fails (just like his army in six battles) (1 mark), but like the spider he is resilient and takes even more care to succeed the seventh time (1 mark).

5 **d** disapproving.

'disapproving' is the only word that is not a synonym for 'disheartened' in this context.

It is important to remember that the negative meaning associated with the prefix dis- must be applied to the root word, in this case 'approve', which is not relevant here.

6 cat: scattered. After their sixth defeat, the Scottish army scattered into the mountains (lines 7–8).

7 ten: fastened. On the seventh attempt, the spider fastened her thread to the beam (line 20).

8 eat: creature. Bruce declared that the creature had taught him a lesson (line 27).

Test 30

(pages 82–83)

1 **a** a potential source of energy in the future.

See line 2 – 'possible new sustainable fuel sources';

b sometimes derived from waste products.

See lines 7–8 – 'even human waste' can be used;

d still being investigated.

See the last sentence of paragraph one.

The references to 'scientists all over the world' (line 1) and 'Research projects around the globe' (line 6) demonstrate that this is not limited to the UK, so option **c** is not correct. Option **e** is also incorrect as biofuels are suggested as 'a long-term alternative to fossil fuels' in line 5, showing that they are not the same as fossil fuels.

2 Seaweed is likely to be grown in:

salt-water lakes and fjords (lines 10–11) (1 mark);

purpose-built harbours (line 11) (1 mark);

vast off-shore pens in the open sea (lines 11–12) (1 mark).

No marks are given for referring to farms, as this does not make it clear they are farms in specific locations in the water.

3 One advantage of seaweed as a fuel is that it grows at a fast rate, so is an easily renewable energy source (see lines 12–13).

4 c meagre

'plentiful' means 'more than sufficient', while 'meagre' means 'lacking in quantity'.

5 The two statements that are definitely true are:

a The process is expensive. See line 18: 'At the moment, the high costs involved limit the scale of production';

c There is a lot of work involved with harvesting seaweed. See line 23: 'very labour-intensive'.

The other options are wrong because there is no reference to seaweed replacing non-renewable sources soon (**b**), scientists are not agreed (**d**) (lines 20–24) and seaweed is not yet used on a large scale (**e**), since line 22 mentions scientists' reservations about large-scale production 'owing to the amount of space required'.

6 MAN: DEMAND, MANAGEABLE

7 TEN: POTENTIAL, INTENSIVE

Test 31
(pages 84–85)

1 c are busy all day long.

See lines 5–6: 'there are many idle hours that have to be whiled away'.

a is true, because it is stated in line 1, 'The life of the guardian of a blazing signpost of the coast is much the same the whole world over.' **b** is shown to be true in lines 2–3, 'Each succeeding day and night brings a similar round of toil, with very little variation.' **d** is shown to be true in lines 6–8, 'On the mainland … loneliness and monotony are not felt so keenly'. **e** is true because line 13 states that the keepers who live on the mainland 'can expend their hours of leisure to advantage'.

2 d nearness

'remoteness' has the opposite meaning, and the other three have unrelated meanings.

3 a bordering

'bordering' means 'being adjacent to', so it is a synonym for 'flanking'.

4 e diligently

'diligently' means 'attentively', so it has the most similar meaning to 'vigilantly'.

5 'The gilt of fascination wears away quickly' means that the visitors to the lighthouse quickly realise that, although it is interesting and may seem romantic and peaceful to be so isolated (1 mark), this is just a good first impression ('gilt' referring to something covered in gold) and the reality is soon obvious to them (1 mark).

6 In an emergency:

they must wait for a ship to come by (1 mark);

communicate by flag signals so the ship knows there is something wrong (1 mark);

if there is a doctor on board, they will come and help (1 mark);

if it is serious, the ship will take the ill person off (1 mark).

7 not: monotonous

8 one: marooned

PUZZLE ANSWERS

Puzzle 1

(page 86)

1 limited (Rationing ensured **limited** supplies were fairly distributed.)

2 entitled (The ration book **entitled** people to certain amounts of rationed foodstuffs.)

3 vitamins (Poorer people were able to access foods richer in minerals and **vitamins** after rationing began.)

4 supplementary (People with additional nutritional needs were given **supplementary** rations.)

5 advice (The Ministry of Food issued **advice** to people about how to use their rations.)

6 broadcast (Some recipes were printed on leaflets or **broadcast** on the radio.)

7 substituted (Sometimes scarce ingredients were **substituted** with more readily available basic commodities.)

8 palates (Some recipes do not sound very appealing to modern **palates**.)

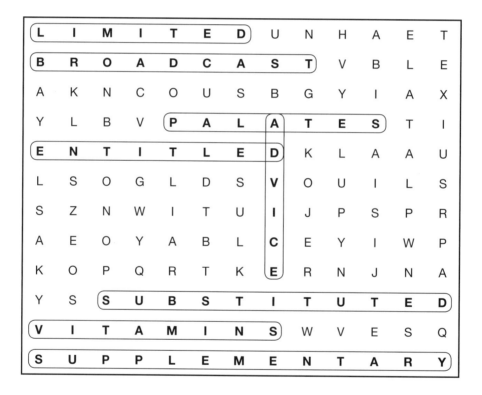

Puzzle 2

(page 87)

silence (the letters also spell 'license', but this is not in Test 8), composed, sound, century, famous, experiment, piano, musical, renowned, objects, noises, minutes, quietly, time, duration, extreme

The word that means 'one hundred years' is 'century'.

Other words with the cent- prefix meaning 'one hundred' could include: centimetre, centigrade, centipede, centilitre, centurion, centennial.

The three words beginning with 'ex' in Test 8 are: extreme, experiment and explored.

Other words beginning with 'ex' could include: exact, expect, expert, excited, examine, excellent.

There are many words that can be made from the letters in the word 'traditionally'. A few possible ones are: it, in, on, rail, tail, trail, diary, daily, rainy, dollar, tailor, tradition.

Puzzle 3

(page 88)

Across: 4 shore; **5** gnawing; **7** mistake; **8** generous; **9** watered; **10** stray

Down: 1 bone; **2** lost; **3** floundered; **6** astute; **7** mangy

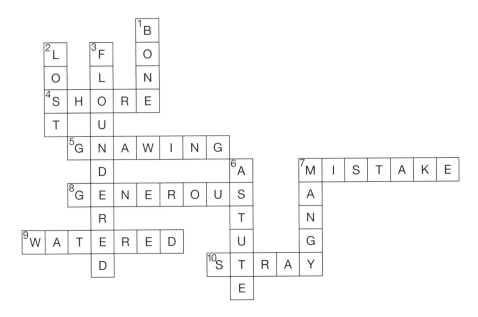

Puzzle 4

(page 89)

Here are some suggested answers, but other answers that work are also acceptable:

free, flee, fled, bled, bred, **brew**

boat, moat, moan, loan, load, **loud**

play, pray, tray, trap, trip, **trim**

fleck, flock, block, black, blank, **blink**

Puzzle 5

(page 90)

rein, rain, reign (has two homophones); **herd**, heard; **hole**, whole; **threw**, through; **knight**, night; **mourning**, morning; **scents**, sense, cents (has two homophones); **maid**, made; **scene**, seen

Puzzle 6

(page 91)

1 evolve; **2** eyesight; **3** habitat; **4** omnivorous; **5** invertebrate; **6** hindrance; **7** armour; **8** litter; **9** similar; **10** threat; **11** extinct; **12** predator

Puzzle 7

(page 92)

First puzzle:

foothills, bright, villages, cold, wooded, mountain, valley, sunny, slopes, morning

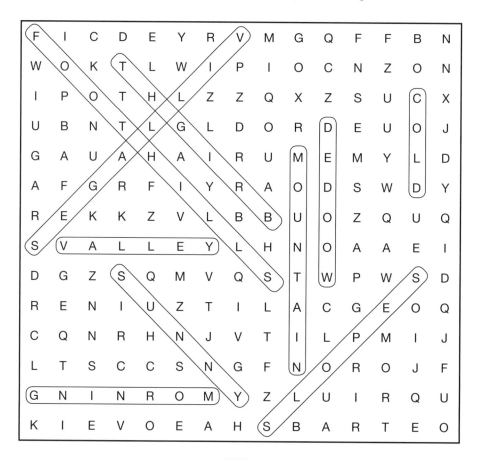

Second puzzle:

vibrations, flashed, fireball, thunderclap, cloud, smoke, burning, airwave, roar, shattered

Puzzle 8

(page 93)

Owls are **unusual** birds. They are nocturnal, which means they are **active during the night**. They are mostly **solitary**, except during the **mating** season. They have **binocular** vision, which allows them to see more and helps them to **locate** prey. They have special feathers adapted for silent **flight**.

They have fourteen vertebrae, which allows **flexibility** in their neck. Mythology says that owls are **wise**, but in fact studies show that although they are adept at hunting, they may be **significantly** worse at **solving problems** than parrots or crows.

Puzzle 9

(page 94)

List 1: tradition, custom, ritual, practice, habit, routine

List 2: lush, verdant, abundant, thriving, prolific, luxuriant

List 3: alarming, frightening, worrying, scary, terrifying, shocking

List 4: rapid, fast, speedy, quick, brisk, prompt

List 5 or 6: giant, huge, enormous, vast

List 5 or 6: absurd, ridiculous, preposterous, ludicrous

4 Explain two ways in which June and December are opposites. ⬭ 2

_____

_____

5 Select the **ONE** word on the right that is most **SIMILAR** in meaning to the word on the left, as used in line 9 of the poem. Underline the correct answer. ⬭ 1

scorched   **a** dry   **b** hot   **c** cut   **d** burnt   **e** sunny

6 Which of the following options best matches the description of the month of October in the poem? Underline the best answer from options **a–e**. ⬭ 1

a a bitter month   **b** a harsh month   **c** a sunny month

d a calm month   **e** a flowery month

7 What is the poet referring to when she says 'Earth must disrobe her' in line 15? ⬭ 1

a the bad weather

b the leaves falling off the trees

c the falling stars

d the fruit on the trees

e the dry earth being blown

8 Read the following paragraph and add **ONE** word from the box to each space so that the paragraph makes sense. Each word can only be used once. ⬭ 8

February	warm	weather	months
different	abundant	rains	June

The poem is about how each of the _____ of the year are

_____. In particular, the _____ varies greatly. For

example, in _____, it often _____ a lot according to the

poem. By contrast, _____ is a very _____ time of year.

August and September are when crops are most _____.

Total ⬭ 16

Test 19

Read the text carefully and answer the questions that follow.

The Tenrec

Tenrecs are small mammals found all over the island of Madagascar and in some parts of mainland Africa. They have evolved in a remarkably similar way to other mammals in many different parts of the world, such as possums in Australia

and hedgehogs in Europe. They are similar to hedgehogs, mice and shrews, with pointy noses and poor eyesight. There are many species of tenrec and they vary in size considerably, depending on the species: the smallest are just a few grams in weight, while the largest – the common tenrec – can weigh up to one kilogram.

Their usual habitat is in forested areas, although the aquatic tenrec, as the name suggests, lives in rivers and streams in its native Madagascar. Tenrecs are omnivorous, meaning they eat vegetation and other animals; in fact, their diet largely consists of invertebrates, which they find by foraging on the forest floor. Their poor eyesight is not a hindrance since they are usually nocturnal, relying heavily on their acute sense of smell and hearing.

While smaller species of tenrec tend to be covered in fur, some of the larger species have evolved to have a covering of spines, similar to hedgehogs and porcupines. In fact, there are species of tenrec known as the lesser and greater hedgehog tenrec. Their spiny armour provides them with protection from predators such as birds of prey and snakes.

Tenrecs give birth to live young, with the size of the litter varying considerably from one to up to thirty young being born at a time, depending on the species.

Despite being one of the world's oldest mammals, the survival of many species of tenrec is now under threat due to the destruction of their forest habitat. Deforestation on the island of Madagascar, involving the clearing of trees by cutting and burning, has resulted in dramatic environmental damage. Unless something is done soon, many species of tenrec may one day become extinct.

1   Explain why the tenrec's poor eyesight is not a problem for it.

_____

_____

Complete each of the following sentences by selecting **ONE** ending from options **a–e** that is the best fit. Underline the correct answer.

2 According to the first paragraph in the text, tenrecs are found:

    a in all parts of Africa

    b only on Madagascar

    c in some parts of Madagascar

    d all over the world

    e on Madagascar and in regions of mainland Africa

3 The tenrec's diet consists of:

    a small mammals   **b** only vegetation   **c** both plants and animals

    d large insects only   **e** birds and snakes

4 Select the **ONE** word on the right that has the most **SIMILAR** meaning to the word on the left, taken from the text. Underline the correct answer.

protection   **a** attack   **b** coat   **c** destruction   **d** defence   **e** threat

5 Read the following paragraph and add **ONE** word from the box to each space so that the paragraph makes sense. There are more words than there are spaces so one will be left out, but each word can only be used once.

threat	island	common	species	covering
mainland	predators	survival	protect	evolved

There are many _____ of tenrec, although they all live either on the

African _____ or the _____ of Madagascar, off the

African coast. The largest tenrec is the _____ tenrec, and these weigh

up to one kilogram. Birds and snakes are among the tenrecs' _____,

but their _____ of spines helps to _____ them.

Sadly, deforestation has destroyed much of their natural habitat and their

_____ is now under _____.

Total 14

Test 20

Read the text carefully and answer the questions that follow.

The Wonderful City of Oz: an extract by L. Frank Baum

Even with eyes protected by the green spectacles, Dorothy and her friends were at first dazzled by the brilliancy of the wonderful City. The streets were lined with beautiful houses all built of green marble and studded everywhere with sparkling emeralds. They walked over a pavement of the same green marble, and where the blocks were joined together were rows of emeralds, set 5 closely, and glittering in the brightness of the sun. The window panes were of green glass; even the sky above the City had a green tint, and the rays of the sun were green.

There were many people – men, women and children – walking about, and these were all dressed in green clothes and had greenish skins. They looked 10 at Dorothy and her strangely assorted company with wondering eyes, and the children all ran away and hid behind their mothers when they saw the Lion; but no one spoke to them. Many shops stood in the street, and Dorothy saw that everything in them was green. Green candy and green pop corn were offered for sale, as well as green shoes, green hats, and green clothes of all sorts. At 15 one place, a man was selling green lemonade, and when the children bought it Dorothy could see that they paid for it with green pennies.

There seemed to be no horses nor animals of any kind; the men carried things around in little green carts, which they pushed before them. Everyone seemed happy and contented and prosperous. 20

The Guardian of the Gates led them through the streets until they came to a big building, exactly in the middle of the City, which was the Palace of Oz, the Great Wizard. There was a soldier before the door, dressed in a green uniform and wearing a long green beard.

"Here are strangers," said the Guardian of the Gates to him, "and they 25 demand to see the Great Oz."

"Step inside," answered the soldier, "and I will carry your message to him."

So they passed through the Palace Gates and were led into a big room with a green carpet and lovely green furniture set with emeralds. The soldier made them all wipe their feet upon a green mat before entering this room, and when 30 they were seated he said politely:

"Please make yourselves comfortable while I go to the door of the Throne Room and tell Oz you are here."

"Thank you," replied the girl; "that is very kind of Oz."

1 How did Dorothy try to stop herself from being dazzled by the sparkling City?

_____

2 According to the first two paragraphs, the City contained many unusual features. Which **ONE** of the following features is **NOT** mentioned in the description of the City? Underline the correct answer from options **a–e**.

a green glass in the windows

b emeralds dotted around the streets and buildings

c green marble pavements

d shops selling green foods

e green rain falling from the green sky

3 Which words or phrases from the text in paragraph two show that the children were afraid?

_____

4 Apart from being green, what else was unusual about the City, according to paragraph three? Underline the correct answer.

a the animals **b** the weather **c** the lack of animals

d the size of the horses **e** the horse-drawn carts

5 Select the **ONE** word on the right that has the most **SIMILAR** meaning to the word on the left, taken from the text. Underline the correct answer.

prosperous **a** happy **b** popular **c** wealthy **d** healthy **e** strange

6 Read the following paragraph and add **ONE** word from the box to each space so that the paragraph makes sense. Each word can only be used once.

furnished	wait	companions	follow	enter	uniform

To enter the Palace, Dorothy and her _____ had to

_____ the Guardian of the Gates. A soldier, whose

_____ was green, allowed them to _____.

The room they were led into was _____ in green too. They were asked

to _____ while the soldier took a message to the Throne Room.

© 2017 Oxford University Press • COPYING STRICTLY PROHIBITED

Time for a break! ★ Go to Puzzle Page 91 →

Total 12

Test 21

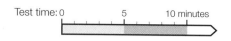

Read the text carefully and answer the questions that follow.

A Meteorite Falls in the Taiga, USSR
Extract from *Space Nomads* by Lincoln LaPaz and Jean LaPaz
The morning of February 12, 1947, dawned cold but bright and sunny in the
wide Ussuri valley of Eastern Siberia. During the early morning hours, the
people in the villages went about their everyday chores as usual. Farmers
fed and watered their livestock, while housewives tidied rooms and fired up
stoves for heating and baking. Miners went to work deep underground. An   **5**
artist seated himself outdoors near his home to make exercise sketches. In
a densely wooded area on the slopes of a nearby mountain range, a logging
crew began a day's timber-cutting.

Suddenly, at 10:35 a.m., an extraordinarily large and brilliant fireball flashed
above the central part of the mountain range. It streaked across the sky in less   **10**
than 5 seconds and disappeared beyond the western foothills of the range.
Then the inhabitants of a wide area heard what seemed to them a mighty
thunderclap followed by a powerful roar like an artillery cannonade. Many
people felt a strong airwave.

For several hours afterward, a large black column of smoke tinged with a   **15**
reddish-rose colour stood above the place of fall. Gradually, this cloud spread
outward, became curved and then zigzag in form, and finally vanished toward
the end of the day.

The flash of the fireball and the loud noises that followed it caused panic
among the farm animals. Cows lowed mournfully and herds of goats scattered   **20**
in every direction, chickens and other fowl squawked in alarm, and dogs ran
whining for shelter or crouched against the legs of their masters.

In the villages, the airwave blew snow off the roofs of houses and other
buildings, while the strong earth-shocks opened windows and made doors
swing ajar. Housewives were dismayed to see glass windowpanes shattered   **25**
in their frames and burning coals and firebrands jolted out of the wood-
burning stoves.

Even deep in the mineshaft, the vibrations in the air were strong enough to
snuff out the miners' lamps, leaving the men in darkness.

On seeing the huge fireball streak across the sky, the artist put aside his   **30**
practice sketch and began a picture of the display before his impressions of it
could fade. His painting of this natural event is now famous. Not only is it on
display in scientific museums all around the world, but a colour reproduction
of it has been issued in Russia as a postage stamp.

1   Complete the following sentence. Underline the correct answer from options **a–e**.

1

The meteor fell:

   a on the afternoon of an autumn day

   b thousands of years ago in Siberia

   c during the morning of a February day in 1947

   d on a hot and sunny morning in Siberia

   e during the night of February 12, 1947

2   Describe **FIVE** of the everyday chores people were doing before the meteor fell.

5

_____

_____

_____

_____

_____

3   The author describes sights, sounds and feelings as the meteor fell. Find **ONE** example for each of these from the text.

3

Sights: _____

Sounds: _____

Feelings: _____

4   How did the artist help record the event? Underline the correct answer from options **a–e.**

1

   a He wrote down what he had seen and sent it to the museum.

   b He took a picture that was put on display.

   c He stopped painting and watched.

   d He painted a picture straightaway before he could forget what he had seen.

   e He decided to make a stamp showing the event.

Total   10

Test 22

Read the text carefully and answer the questions that follow.

Experience: I own the world's fastest tortoise

As told to Chris Broughton, from the *Guardian* newspaper, 2 October 2015

When Bertie gets going, there's no stopping him – he charges off like a big clockwork toy. We once put down a bowl of his favourite food, strawberries, to tempt him in a certain direction and he charged straight over the top of it and kept going. Neither Marco nor I had ever owned a tortoise before, so we didn't have anything to compare him with.   **5**

We did some research and started conducting our own trials. A visit to the Guinness World Records website told us that the fastest recognised tortoise was Charlie, who had covered 18 feet in 43.7 seconds at the National Tortoise Championships at Tickhill, South Yorkshire, in 1977. We measured Bertie's speed over the same distance and, to our astonishment, he beat Charlie's   **10** record comfortably. Thinking we had made a mistake, we turned him round and timed him again, with the same result. There was only one thing for it: we were going to have to take this to a higher authority.

The criteria we received back from Guinness were quite specific and very strict. We had to recreate the conditions of the previous record exactly,   **15** building an 18ft track with a one-in-12 gradient, so Bertie would be racing slightly uphill, just as Charlie had. We needed an architect there to ensure the gradient was exactly right and two official timekeepers, loaned by our local football club, Sunderland. There was a vet present, too, to ensure Bertie was all right, and all these witnesses had to give statements.   **20**

The morning of the attempt was pretty nerve-racking. We didn't know what sort of mood Bertie would be in. He seemed unfazed, though, as we brought him into the room where the experts were waiting. It was dominated by the track, a self-contained trough with a chequered finishing line at the top. Bertie performed well on a couple of trial runs, so we decided to go for it.   **25**

As he was placed on the starting line, Bertie's legs were already sweeping the air. He pounded up the track, clawed feet stomping as the onlookers egged him on: "Come on, Bertie! Come on, son! Final stretch, lad!" There were cheers as he crossed the finishing line and, true to form, kept going.

Bertie hadn't just beaten the record, he'd smashed it. His time was 21.47   **30** seconds – half Charlie's time. Given that he was still raring to go, we let him run again and he shaved almost another two seconds off his own record: 19.59 seconds, faster than we'd ever measured him.

We were overjoyed, but we didn't tell anyone, other than close friends and family. We had to wait for the next *Guinness Book of Records* to be announced. Soon after the record was measured, a representative from Guinness visited to hand over the certificate. As Marco held him up for the photographers, Bertie responded by urinating on his feet. I don't know if it was the excitement – tortoise emotions can be hard to read.

> ## LOCATING INFORMATION
> This text is taken from a real newspaper and recounts a true story. Texts such as this are usually structured in chronological order. Use this to help you locate the answers to the questions more easily.

1 Underline the correct answer from options **a–e** to complete the following sentence. Bertie is described as being 'like a big clockwork toy' in paragraph one because he:

   a goes very fast   **b** looks like a child's toy tortoise   **c** goes in the wrong direction

   d keeps on going regardless of what is in his way   **e** runs off in all directions

        1

2 Find **TWO** pieces of evidence from paragraph two that show that the owners were surprised by Bertie's record attempt.

        2

_____

_____

3 Which of the following options was **NOT** among the criteria for achieving the Guinness record attempt? Underline the correct answer from options **a–e**.

   a identical track to record holder's   **b** slope checked   **c** time checked by officials

   d use of a special stopwatch   **e** Bertie's welfare checked by vet

        1

4 Describe what sort of mood Bertie seemed to be in on the morning of the attempt.

        2

_____

_____

5 Underline the answer from options **a–e** that has the most **SIMILAR** meaning to 'egged him on' in lines 27–28.

        1

   a encouraged him   **b** threw eggs at him   **c** teased him

   d ran with him   **e** gave him treats

Total   7

Test 23

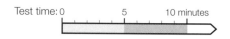

Read the text carefully and answer the questions that follow.

The Footprints in the Dew
Extract from Chapter V, *Tom's Midnight Garden* by Philippa Pearce

There is a time, between night and day, when landscapes sleep. Only the
early riser sees the hour; or the all-night traveller, letting up the blind of his
railway-carriage window, will look out on a rushing landscape of stillness, in
which trees and bushes and plants stand immobile and breathless in sleep –
wrapped in sleep, as the traveller himself wrapped his body in his great-coat   5
or his rug the night before.

This grey, still hour before morning was the time in which Tom walked into his
garden. He had come down the stairs and along the hall to the garden door at
midnight; but when he opened that door and stepped out into the garden, the
time was much later. All night – moonlit or swathed in darkness – the garden   10
had stayed awake; now, after that night-long vigil, it had dozed off.

The green of the garden was greyed over with dew; indeed, all its colours were
gone until the touch of sunrise. The air was still, and the tree-shapes crouched
down upon themselves. One bird spoke; and there was a movement when an
awkward parcel of feathers dislodged itself from the tall fir-tree at the corner   15
of the lawn, seemed for a second to fall and then at once was swept up and
along, outspread, on a wind that never blew, to another, farther tree: an owl. It
wore the ruffled, dazed appearance of one who has been up all night.

Tom began to walk round the garden, on tiptoe. At first he took the outermost
paths, gravelled and box-edged, intending to map for himself their farthest   20
extent. Then he broke away impatiently on a cross-path. It tunnelled through
the gloom of yew-trees arching overhead from one side, and hazel nut stubs
from the other: ahead was a grey-green triangle of light where the path must
come out into the open again. Underfoot the earth was soft with the humus
of last year's rotted leaves. As he slipped along, like a ghost, Tom noticed,   25
through gaps in the yew-trees on his right, the flick of lighter colour than the
yew: dark – light – dark – light – dark … The lighter colour, he realized, was the
back of the house that he was glimpsing, and he must be passing behind the
line of yew-trees that faced it across the lawn.

He came out by the asparagus beds of the kitchen-garden – so he found them   30
later to be. Beyond their long, grave-like mounds was a dark oblong – a pond.
At the end of the pond, and overlooking it, stood an octagonal summer-house
with an arcaded base and stone steps up to its door. The summer-house, like
the rest of the garden, was asleep on its feet.

Beyond the pond and the summer-house was another path, meandering in idle   35
curves. On the other side of this path was a stretch of wilderness, and then a hedge.

1 To complete the following sentence, underline the best answer from options **a–e**.

CLOSE READING

If a question asks for the 'best' answer, this suggests that there may be more than one plausible answer given but one is more accurate or nearest to the text. Find the relevant passage of text and read it again closely.

The opening paragraph mainly describes:

a the garden at midnight

b a sleepy traveller

c a long train journey

d a foggy morning

e how places look at dawn

2 Underline the correct answer from options **a–e**.

'night-long vigil' in line 11 suggests the garden:

a was like someone who was wide awake

b was like a tired person

c was like a person who had kept watch

d was in darkness

e looked grey and miserable

3 In paragraph three, what kind of bird does the author describe?

_____

4 Describe **THREE** things in paragraph three that the reader can tell about the bird's behaviour or appearance.

_____

_____

_____

5 Select the **ONE** word on the right that has the most **OPPOSITE** meaning to the word on the left, taken from the text. Underline the correct answer.

farthest   **a** away   **b** distance   **c** beside   **d** beyond   **e** nearest

6 Select the **TWO** words on the right that are **NOT SIMILAR** in meaning to the word on the left, taken from the text. Underline the correct answers.

gloom   **a** darkness   **b** shadows   **c** dawn   **d** murkiness   **e** cloudy

Total   8

Test 24

Read the text carefully and answer the questions that follow.

The History of Tap Dancing

Tap dancing is a form of dance in which the dancer wears special shoes that
have a metal plate on the toe and heel. By striking the floor with their feet
in different ways, the dancer creates intricate and often very fast rhythms in
time to the music. Now part of mainstream dance culture and seen on theatre
stages the world over, its roots lie in an altogether different past. **5**

Although often referred to as an American dance form, tap has its origins
in African drumming traditions. Its development is deeply rooted in the
social and cultural injustices of 19th-century America, particularly the slave
trade. Africans who had been brought to America as slaves brought with
them religious and cultural traditions which involved rhythmical dancing and **10**
drumming. Where possible, they continued to practise and uphold these
customs, despite their oppression. The slaveholders, who were worried that
this might lead to revolt, tried to control this drumming. However, this only led
to slaves finding new ways to connect and protest, and they transferred the
drumming of rhythmic patterns from their hands to their feet. Tap was born. **15**

Over time, this dancing became combined with the British and Irish clog-dancing
tradition, which had also made its way across the Atlantic and had its roots in
working-class culture. A style of dancing called 'Buck and Wing' was borne out
of this fusion and this paved the way for the emergence of modern tap.

By 1928, tap dancing was referred to for the first time as a genre in its own **20**
right and gradually became established as a more mainstream form of dance.
Although the form declined in popularity during the fifties and sixties, when
rock and roll was at its peak, there has been a steady revival of tap dancing
since. Nowadays, tap is a style offered by many dance schools and there
is even a rise in adults taking up tap dancing for the first time as a fitness **25**
activity. There are many variations of the style, but all share a common feature
of using a syncopated (or off-beat) pattern and a wealth of fancy footwork.

1 Which **THREE** of the following are involved in tap dancing, according to the first
paragraph? Underline the correct answers from options **a–e**. 3

    a complicated rhythmic patterns

    b clapping intricate rhythms

    c metal toe and heel plates

    d hitting the feet on the ground

    e elaborate drumming

2 Explain what is meant by the phrase 'seen on theatre stages the world over' in lines 4–5, referring to the text.

_____

3 Underline the best answer from options **a–e**.

The words 'uphold these customs' in lines 11–12 mean:

a share their beliefs

b create a new dance

c remember the past

d develop a habit

e maintain a tradition

4 Read the following paragraph and add **ONE** word from the box to each space so that the paragraph makes sense. There are more words than there are spaces so one will be left out, but each word can only be used once.

> communities   originated   tradition   feet   alternative   restricted   pattern

Tap dancing _____ in America, but it developed from the

_____ of African drumming among slave _____.

When their use of drums was _____, they developed an

_____ way of creating complex rhythms using the

_____.

Select the **TWO** odd words out on each line. Select your answers by underlining **TWO** of the options **a–e**.

5 **a** revolt   **b** protest   **c** retreat   **d** rebel   **e** panic

6 **a** custom   **b** variation   **c** ritual   **d** convention   **e** dance

7 Underline the word on the right that is **CLOSEST** in meaning to the word from the text, on the left.

fusion   **a** style   **b** custom   **c** amalgamation   **d** performance   **e** emergence

Total   14

Read the text carefully and answer the questions that follow.

The Miracle Plant

Years of research had gone into developing the seeds that Nina now held in her palm. Small, brown, inconspicuous, almost dust-like seeds that held so much potential. Miracle plants. Finding just the right combination of strength and resistance to disease had been a challenge for the scientists, but finally they had done it. When planted, these tiny pockets of life should spring forth   5 in abundance, weaving themselves into a crop of plants that had the capacity not only to provide a staple food for millions of people, but could also be used as a fuel when harvested and allowed to ferment. But the greatest miracle of all was the speed at which they grew.

The whole lab seemed to hold its breath as Nina dropped the seeds into   10 the tray her colleague had prepared with the specifically designed soil. If their estimates were correct, the seeds would start to germinate in a matter of minutes, breaking all known records and assuring them of a place in the history books. Tension mixed with anticipation filled the air. With crops that grew that fast, who knew what they could achieve?   15

As the huge stopwatch on the screen above their heads began to count up, all eyes were on the seed tray. Slowly at first, then more rapidly, specks of bright green began to appear on the surface of the soil. The scientists applauded. Curling outwards and then stretching up, spindly stalks began to extend out of the tray. Each one was becoming stronger and more like a limb of a   20 huge creature before their very eyes, and along the length of the stalk grew spiky hairs, as sharp as needles. The assembled crowd gasped. The ever-growing tentacles reached out towards them, pulling and tugging. Amazement turned to panic as a forest of fleshy vegetation filled the lab. In creating the long-awaited miracle plant, they seemed to have unleashed something   25 unstoppable. Powerless, they watched as their years of work grew into a nightmare in a few short moments.

1 Underline the best answer from options **a–e** to complete the following sentence.

The miracle seeds had:

a taken years to grow

b been found in a lab

c taken scientists a long time to develop

d been designed to cure diseases

e been found by Nina in a palm tree

2 Explain what is meant by the phrase 'tiny pockets of life' in line 5, referring to the text.

2

_____

_____

1

3 Underline the correct answer from options **a–e** to complete the following sentence.

The phrase 'a staple food' in line 7 means:

a a food that is eaten all over the world

b a miracle food that has never been grown before

c a food that is eaten regularly and forms the major part of people's diets

d a food that is in short supply everywhere

e a food that can supplement other foods

3

4 According to paragraph one, what **THREE** unusual aspects make the plant a 'miracle'?

_____

_____

_____

2

Underline the best answer from options **a–e** to complete the following sentences.

5 The words 'The whole lab seemed to hold its breath' in line 10 show that:

a everyone was breathless

b everyone was excited

c someone knew the plant was going to run wild

d everyone was nervous and excited

e everyone thought Nina would do it wrong

6 The word 'limb' in line 20 suggests it:

a was like an arm or leg   **b** was like a giant   **c** had toes

d grew a face   **e** could walk

1

7 Underline the word on the right that is **OPPOSITE** in meaning to the word from the text, on the left.

unleashed   **a** pulled   **b** untied   **c** created   **d** witnessed   **e** restrained

Total | 10

Test 26

Read the text carefully and answer the questions that follow.

The Fjords
What is a fjord?
A fjord is a long, narrow inlet of water between high mountains in a glacial valley.

How are fjords formed?
When **glaciers** develop, they gradually move, eroding the rock beneath to
carve away deep troughs. As the ice melts, steep-sided U-shaped valleys   **5**
remain: glacial valleys. If sea levels rise, these glacial valleys fill with sea water
and are known as fjords.

Where are fjords found?
Fjords are found where there are glacial valleys below sea level: parts of
Canada, New Zealand and even Chile. However, perhaps the places best   **10**
known for their fjords are Norway and other parts of **Scandinavia**. In fact,
Norway is sometimes called 'The Land of the Fjords' and the word 'fjord'
originates from an ancient Norse word meaning a 'water body'.

What is a fjord like?
A deep, calm body of water surrounded by dramatic, rugged mountains   **15**
makes a fjord one of the most spectacular and peaceful places on Earth. Huge
waterfalls tumble over the steep sides and splash into the clear icy depths
below. In many fjords, there are islands and rocky outcrops jutting into the
main body of water. Some are inhabited; others not.

One of the most famous fjords is Geirangerfjord, in Norway. It is a protected   **20**
UNESCO World Heritage Site (a place that is recognised by the United Nations
Educational, Scientific and Cultural Organization for its unique importance).
Every year, in the late spring and summer months, many tourists visit
Geirangerfjord to witness this breathtaking landscape, savouring the clear,
unpolluted air and velvet green mountainsides. The easiest way to get there is   **25**
by boat, with the majority of visitors arriving by cruise ship. Shops, cafés and
visitor centres have been built in the small town, along the shoreline, to cater
for this influx, and much of the local economy is driven by tourism. In winter,
the bitter cold weather limits access to the fjord via either land or sea, with
snow and ice blocking many routes in, and the remaining population is small.   **30**

Glacier – a mass of dense ice formed when the snow and ice builds up and
becomes compacted
Scandinavia – the countries in and around the northernmost part of Europe,
including Denmark, Finland, Sweden and Norway

1 Underline the best answer from options **a–e** to complete the following sentence.

Glacial valleys are formed when:

a water washes away the rock

b ice wears away the rock

c a glacier floats towards the land

d rocks gradually crumble away

e the sea water gradually dissolves the mountainside

Select the **ONE** word on the right that has the most **SIMILAR** meaning to the words on the left, taken from the text. Underline the correct answer.

2 trough   **a** container   **b** stream   **c** gully   **d** fence   **e** flow

3 originates   **a** translates   **b** spreads   **c** language   **d** appears   **e** derives

4 List **THREE NATURAL** features that you might expect to find in or near a fjord, according to the text.

_____

_____

_____

5 Which of the following options is closest in meaning to the word 'unique' in line 22? Underline the correct answer from options **a–e**.

a beautiful

b clear and natural

c at risk

d unlike anything else

e inspirational

6 Which word in the final paragraph means the arrival of a large number of people?

_____

7 Explain why Geirangerfjord is busier in spring and summer.

_____

Total   9

Test 27

Read the text carefully and answer the questions that follow.

Birds by Carton Moore Park

The Magpie

The magpie is not, as a rule, on good terms with his neighbours. He is very noisy, very mischievous, and very quarrelsome, and is not above stealing eggs from the nests of other birds. No doubt he clears the fields of a great number of grubs and slugs, but he does so much damage in the poultry-yard that he always goes the other way when he sees the farmer coming. His nest is built very cunningly of sticks and clay, and he surrounds it with sharp thorny twigs to keep out robbers like himself.

5

The Flamingo

The flamingo is most happy standing on one leg in a foot or two of water. There he waits patiently for any fish that may come his way. His colour may be pink or scarlet according to the part of the world in which he is born; and when he is standing motionless on the look-out for fish, his red body and long legs give him quite a military appearance—like a soldier at attention. The flamingo prefers a warm climate, and by moving from place to place he manages to enjoy a continual summer-time.

10

15

The Vulture

The vulture is a very useful bird, but he would not make a pleasant pet. His home is in the sunny lands of the south, where he is always very busy in tidying up for Dame Nature. When any poor animal is killed or dies of old age the news seems to spread like magic, for although not a single bird may be in sight, in the course of a few minutes vultures come flocking up from all sides. And they never leave their banquet until they have eaten up everything but the bones.

20

The Eagle

The eagle has long been regarded as the King of Birds, just as the lion is spoken of as the King of Beasts. There are some who say that he is not worthy of this honour, but certainly few of his subjects would care to fight him for the crown, for he has a remarkably strong beak, and his feet are armed with the sharpest of claws. Soaring high up in the air, he swoops down on his prey like a thunderbolt from the sky, and carries it off to his nest on some rocky cliff or steep mountain side. Small birds, rabbits, lambs, and fawns all help to fill the eagle's larder.

25

30

LOCATING INFORMATION

When answering questions on a text like this, use subheadings to locate the relevant section. Then scan the section to locate the relevant information.

Select the **ONE** word on the right that has the most **SIMILAR** meaning to the words on the left, taken from the text. Underline the correct answer.

1 quarrelsome   **a** naughty   **b** argumentative   **c** loud   **d** fierce   **e** sly

2 cunningly   **a** deviously   **b** slowly   **c** cleverly   **d** often   **e** nastily

3 Underline the correct answer from options **a–e** to complete the following sentence.

The flamingo's appearance is compared to:

a a soldier in battle   **b** a red hot flame   **c** a summer's day

d a soldier in a red uniform   **e** a pink fish

4 Explain how the vulture 'tidies up'.

_____

5 Which **ONE** of the following statements about the eagle is **TRUE**, according to the final paragraph? Underline the correct answer from options **a–e**.

a He is stronger than the lion.

b He has the title 'King of Beasts'.

c He has recently earned the title 'King of Birds'.

d Some smaller animals carry things to his larder for him.

e He can swoop down quickly to catch his prey.

6 Read the following paragraph and add **ONE** word from the box to each space so that the paragraph makes sense. There are more words than there are spaces so some will be left out, but each word can only be used once.

magpie	colour	pleasant	companions	vulture	follow
steals	enter	causes	helpful	dead	flamingo

Although the _____ may be considered _____,

eating _____ animals is not very _____. The

_____ is not well liked either: other birds do not like him because

he _____ their eggs and farmers do not like him because of the

damage he _____. Perhaps the most likeable bird in the text is the

_____, owing to its attractive _____.

Total   14

Test 28

Read the text carefully and answer the questions that follow.

Extract from *A Christmas Carol* by Charles Dickens

When Scrooge awoke it was so dark that, looking out of bed, he could scarcely distinguish the transparent window from the opaque walls of his chamber. He was endeavouring to pierce the darkness with his ferret eyes, when the chimes of a neighbouring church struck the four quarters. So he listened for the hour.   **5**

To his great astonishment, the heavy bell went on from six to seven, and from seven to eight, and regularly up to twelve; then stopped. Twelve! It was past two when he went to bed. The clock was wrong. An icicle must have got into the works. Twelve!

He touched the spring of his repeater, to correct this most preposterous clock.   **10**
Its rapid little pulse beat twelve, and stopped.

"Why, it isn't possible," said Scrooge, "that I can have slept through a whole day and far into another night. It isn't possible that anything has happened to the sun, and this is twelve at noon!"

The idea being an alarming one, he scrambled out of bed, and groped his   **15**
way to the window. He was obliged to rub the frost off with the sleeve of his dressing-gown before he could see anything; and could see very little then. All he could make out was that it was still very foggy and extremely cold, and that there was no noise of people running to and fro, and making a great stir, as there unquestionably would have been if night had beaten off bright day, and   **20**
taken possession of the world …

Scrooge went to bed again, and thought, and thought, and thought it over and over, and could make nothing of it. The more he thought, the more perplexed he was; and, the more he endeavoured not to think, the more he thought.

Find the missing **FIVE**-letter word in each question that needs to be added to these words from the extract.   (3)

1   DI _ _ _ _ _ UISH

2   TRAN _ _ _ _ _ NT

3   UN _ _ _ _ _ IONABLY

4 Underline the **TWO** answers that could **NOT** complete the sentence correctly from options **a–e**.

When Scrooge woke up:

a he could see bright light shining through the window

b he peered into the darkness

c he tried to listen to hear what time it was

d he saw a ferret running across his chamber

e he could hardly see the window

5 Which of the words from options **a–e** is **NOT** a synonym for the given word, taken from the text? Underline the correct answer.

preposterous   **a** absurd   **b** ridiculous   **c** wrong
                  d ludicrous   **e** nonsensical

> **CLOSE READING**
> Scan the text to find the given word. Read the sentences around it to help understand the word's meaning in this context.

6 Underline the correct answer from options **a–e** to complete the following sentence.

The words 'groped his way to the window' in lines 15–16 suggest that Scrooge:

a could not walk very well because he kept tripping over his dressing gown

b had to cling onto things to find where he was going in the dark

c did not want to get out of bed

d was desperate to see out of the window

e was very unsteady on his feet because he was an old man

7 Using the information in lines 16–21, explain what Scrooge does at the window.

_____

_____

8 What does the repetition of the words 'and thought, and thought, and thought' in line 22 tell the reader about Scrooge?

_____

9 Select the **ONE** word on the right that has the most **SIMILAR** meaning to the word on the left, taken from the text. Underline the correct answer.

possession   **a** advantage   **b** delight   **c** ownership   **d** present   **e** pride

Total 10

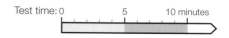
Read the text carefully and answer the questions that follow.

Bruce and the Spider

There was once a king of Scotland whose name was Robert Bruce. He had need to be both brave and wise, for the times in which he lived were wild and rude. The King of England was at war with him and had led a great army into Scotland to drive him out of the land.

Battle after battle had been fought. Six times had Bruce led his brave little   **5** army against his foes; and six times had his men been beaten and driven into flight. At last, his army was scattered, and he was forced to hide himself in the woods and in lonely places among the mountains.

One rainy day, Bruce lay on the ground under a rude shed, listening to the patter of the drops on the roof above him. He was tired and sick at heart, and   **10** ready to give up all hope. It seemed to him that there was no use for him to try to do anything more.

As he lay thinking, he saw a spider over his head, making ready to weave her web. He watched her as she toiled slowly and with great care. Six times she tried to throw her frail thread from one beam to another, and six times it fell short.   **15**

"Poor thing!" said Bruce. "You, too, know what it is to fail."

But the spider did not lose hope with the sixth failure. With still more care, she made ready to try for the seventh time. Bruce almost forgot his own troubles as he watched her swing herself out upon the slender line. Would she fail again? No! The thread was carried safely to the beam and fastened there.   **20**

"I, too, will try a seventh time!" cried Bruce.

He arose and called his men together. He told them of his plans and sent them out with messages of cheer to his disheartened people. Soon there was an army of brave Scottish men around him. Another battle was fought, and the King of England was glad to go back into his own country.   **25**

I have heard it said that, after that day, no one by the name of Bruce would ever hurt a spider. The lesson that the little creature had taught the king was never forgotten.

Underline the correct answer from options **a–e** to complete the following sentences.

1   The word 'foes' in line 6 means:

   a armies   **b** wishes   **c** enemies   **d** friends   **e** neighbours

2 In the story of Bruce and the spider:

   a Robert the Bruce was king of England

   b the English king was trying to take power in Scotland

   c the Scottish had a bigger army than the English

   d the English and Scottish armies were fighting in England

   e Robert the Bruce had led his army into England

READING CAREFULLY
Read each of the statements carefully and eliminate the ones you can be sure about first.

3 Describe how Bruce was feeling when he was forced into hiding, **BEFORE** he sees the spider. Refer to paragraph three in your answer.

(2)

_____

_____

(2)

4 How does the spider inspire Bruce?

_____

_____

5 Which of the words from options **a–e** is **NOT SIMILAR** in meaning to the given word, taken from the text? Underline the correct answer.

(1)

disheartened

   a discouraged   **b** demoralised   **c** deterred   **d** disapproving   **e** dispirited

Find the **THREE**-letter word that is needed to complete each word so that each sentence makes sense. The missing three letters must make a word.

(3)

6 After their sixth defeat, the Scottish army s_____tered into the mountains.

7 On the seventh attempt, the spider fas_____ed her thread to the beam.

8 Bruce declared that the cr_____ure had taught him a lesson.

Total (10)

Read the text carefully and answer the questions that follow.

Seaweed Power: energy of the future?

With the ever-increasing demand for energy, scientists all over the world
are exploring possible new sustainable fuel sources. Biofuels – fuels that
are obtained from a biological process, often involving the decay of organic
matter – offer many significant benefits that researchers are seeking to exploit
further in order to provide a long-term alternative to the use of fossil fuels.   5
Research projects around the globe, including in the UK, have been set up to
investigate how products, such as corn, used vegetable oil and even human
waste, can be utilised to generate a usable form of energy.

One such research project involves the possibility of using harvested seaweed
as a source of energy. Seaweed is grown in huge 'farms' situated in salt-water   10
lakes and fjords, purpose-built harbours and vast off-shore pens in the open
sea. The seaweed, which is not actually a plant but a kind of algae, grows
rapidly. This rate of growth makes it ideal as a renewable fuel source, since
the seaweed beds can be restocked regularly, giving a plentiful and reliable
supply. The harvested seaweed is left to ferment, which results in ethanol   15
being produced. This is a kind of alcohol that can be used as a fuel source to
power cars and other vehicles.

At the moment, the high costs involved limit the scale of production and it is not
yet clear whether growing seaweed to use in this way is a viable and realistic
alternative to traditional non-renewable energy sources. While some researchers   20
have claimed that a large part of the world's energy supply could be provided
in this way, others foresee potential difficulties owing to the amount of space
required and the fact that seaweed farming is very labour-intensive.

What is clear, however, is that on our crowded planet, the demand for clean,
renewable energy sources is a pressing one and that manageable solutions   25
must be found to ensure that future generations can have the energy that they
need without causing further damage to the Earth and its atmosphere.

SUMMARISING TEXTS

In non-fiction texts, it can be useful to quickly summarise what each paragraph is about as you
read. This can help you locate the correct section when answering.

1 Underline the **THREE** correct answers from options **a–e**. ⬭ 1

Biofuels are:

a a potential source of energy in the future

b sometimes derived from waste products

c only being researched in the UK

d still being investigated

e the same as fossil fuels

2 Write down **THREE** places where seaweed is likely to be grown for fuel. ⬭ 3

_____

_____

_____

3 Explain **ONE** advantage of using seaweed as a source of fuel. ⬭ 1

_____

4 Select the **ONE** word on the right that is most **OPPOSITE** in meaning to the word on the left, from line 14 in the text. Underline the correct answer. ⬭ 1

plentiful   **a** many   **b** large   **c** meagre   **d** bountiful   **e** frequent

5 Which **TWO** of the following statements about the use of seaweed as fuel are definitely **TRUE**, according to the third paragraph? Underline the correct answers from options **a–e**. ⬭ 1

a The process is expensive.

b It will replace non-renewable energy sources soon.

c There is a lot of work involved with harvesting seaweed.

d All researchers are agreed on its usefulness.

e It is already being used on a large scale.

Find the missing **THREE** letters that complete these words. The three letters must make a word. The same three letters are used for both words. ⬭ 2

6 DE __ __ __ D   __ __ __ AGEABLE

7 PO __ __ __ TIAL   IN __ __ __ SIVE

Total ⬭ 9

Read the text carefully and answer the questions that follow.

The Lightkeeper and his Life

The life of the guardian of a blazing signpost of the coast is much the same the
whole world over. It is unavoidably monotonous under the best conditions. Each
succeeding day and night brings a similar round of toil, with very little variation.
There are the same duties to be performed in strict accordance with routine and,
under normal circumstances, there are many idle hours that have to be whiled   5
away as best one can. On the mainland, especially in the south of England,
France, Germany and the United States, the loneliness and monotony are not
felt so keenly by the wardens of the light, as in many instances they are in close
proximity to ports and towns, where a little welcome relaxation may be obtained
during the rest spells; while in the summer evenings, if the lighthouse should be   10
only a few miles away from civilisation, visitors are frequent. Again, the keepers,
as a rule, live with their families in cosy solid buildings, and, having a stretch of
garden flanking their homes, can expend their hours of leisure to advantage.

On the isolated, lonely rock, however, the conditions are vastly different. The
average person, when regarding on a calm day the tall slim outline of a tower   15
rising from the water, is apt to regard the life of those responsible for keeping
the light going as one enveloped in romance and peace, far removed from the
trials and worries of the maelstrom of civilisation. But twenty-four hours on
one of these beacons completely dispels all romantic impressions. The gilt of
fascination wears away quickly, and the visitor recognises only too forcibly the   20
terrible desolation of it all, and admires the little band of men who watch vigilantly
over the deep for the guidance of those who go down to the sea in ships.

The keepers of such stations are marooned as completely as any
castaway on a barren island. In many instances, they cannot
even signal to the shore. If anything should go wrong, they
must wait until a ship comes in sight to communicate their   25
tidings by flag signals. If the call is urgent, say for illness, and
the passing boat carries a doctor, she will heave to and, if
conditions permit, will launch a boat to carry the medical man
to the rock to administer aid. If it is a
matter of life or death, the ship will   30
take the man off.

1 Underline **ONE** answer that is **NOT** correct from options **a–e**.

1

According to the text, lighthouse keepers:

a do almost the same job all over the world

b must work hard, doing the same things everyday

c are busy all day long

d on the mainland are not as isolated

e may be able to use their free time to do hobbies

Which word on the right is **SIMILAR** in meaning to the word on the left, taken from the text? Underline the correct answer from options **a–e**.

3

2 proximity   **a** seaside   **b** tower   **c** wrong   **d** nearness   **e** remoteness

3 flanking   **a** bordering   **b** growing   **c** decorating   **d** spacing   **e** keeping

4 vigilantly   **a** angrily   **b** slowly   **c** forcibly   **d** slightly   **e** diligently

5 Explain what the words 'The gilt of fascination wears away quickly' in lines 19–20 mean.

2

_____

_____

6 Using the information in the third paragraph, explain what happens at remote lighthouses in the case of an emergency.

4

_____

_____

_____

_____

Find the **THREE**-letter word that is needed to complete each word so that each sentence makes sense. The missing three letters must make a word.

2

7 The job of a lighthouse keeper can be very mo_____onous.

8 Lighthouse keepers whose lighthouses are on isolated rocks in the sea are

completely maro_____d.

Total   12

Puzzle 1

Missing Letters

In each of the following sentences about wartime recipes, there is a word missing. The words are also hidden in the wordsearch below. Find the words in the wordsearch and use them to complete the sentences.

1 Rationing ensured _____ supplies were fairly distributed.

2 The ration book _____ people to certain amounts of rationed foodstuffs.

3 Poorer people were able to access foods richer in minerals and _____ after rationing began.

4 People with additional nutritional needs were given _____ rations.

5 The Ministry of Food issued _____ to people about how to use their rations.

6 Some recipes were printed on leaflets or _____ on the radio.

7 Sometimes scarce ingredients were _____ with more readily available basic commodities.

8 Some recipes do not sound very appealing to modern _____.

L	I	M	I	T	E	D	U	N	H	A	E	T
B	R	O	A	D	C	A	S	T	V	B	L	E
A	K	N	C	O	U	S	B	G	Y	I	A	X
Y	L	B	V	P	A	L	A	T	E	S	T	I
E	N	T	I	T	L	E	D	K	L	A	A	U
L	S	O	G	L	D	S	V	O	U	I	L	S
S	Z	N	W	I	T	U	I	J	P	S	P	R
A	E	O	Y	A	B	L	C	E	Y	I	W	P
K	O	P	Q	R	T	K	E	R	N	J	N	A
Y	S	S	U	B	S	T	I	T	U	T	E	D
V	I	T	A	M	I	N	S	V	E	E	S	Q
S	U	P	P	L	E	M	E	N	T	A	R	Y

86

Puzzle 2

Anagrams

An anagram is a word with the letters out of order. Unscramble the words below, taken from Test 8.

liecsne _____

decpmsoo _____

ndsuo _____

ntcryeu _____

sofaum _____

ximtpeeren _____

aonpi _____

csmliua _____

nrwdeeno _____

tsojcbe _____

essnoi _____

esnutmi _____

tuelqiy _____

meti _____

atdinour _____

eeemxtr _____

One of the words you have made means 'one hundred years'. Which word is it?

_____

How many other words can you find that have the same prefix as this word?

_____

How many words can you find that begin with 'ex'? There are three in Test 8! How many more can you find?

_____

_____

How many words with two or more letters can you make using the letters in the word 'traditionally'?

_____

_____

_____

Puzzle 3 — Vocabulary Crossword

Find the word for each clue in *The Dog and his Reflection* (Test 11) to complete the crossword.
Think about possible words, then scan the text to locate the one that is in the text.

Across

4 The edge of a body of water (5)

5 Chewing (7)

7 Error (7)

8 Kind or charitable (8)

9 Salivated (7)

10 An animal without a home (5)

Down

1 A part of the skeleton (4)

2 The opposite of found (4)

3 Struggled (10)

6 A synonym for clever (6)

7 With scruffy fur (5)

Puzzle 4

Word Ladders

Change one letter at a time to create new words until you reach the bottom of the ladder.
The first one has already been done as an example.

slow
blow
brow
crow
crew
drew

free
brew

boat
loud

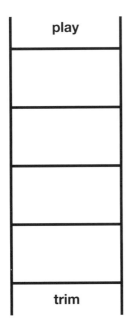

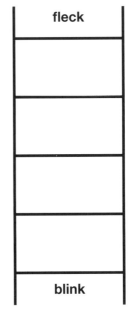

Puzzle 5

Homophones

A homophone is a word that sounds the same as another but has a different spelling. Write a homophone for each word. Below each word, write a sentence to show the correct meaning. The first one has been done for you. The missing homophones can all be found in Test 16.

weather	whether
The match was cancelled due to the weather.	I didn't know whether to go.
rein	_____
herd	_____
hole	_____
threw	_____
knight	_____
mourning	_____
scents	_____
maid	_____
scene	_____

Two words in the list have **two** homophones. What are they?

_____

Puzzle 6 Meanings and Missing Letters

Read the definitions below and fill in the missing letters to make the correct words, which are all taken from Test 19.

1 To gradually change or develop over time

___ v ___ ___ ___ ___

2 The ability to see

e ___ ___ ___ ___ ___ ___ t

3 The environment where something lives

___ ___ ___ ___ ___ a t

4 Describes something that eats plants and animals

___ m ___ ___ ___ ___ ___ ___ ___ s

5 An animal without a backbone

___ ___ v e ___ ___ ___ ___ ___ ___ ___ ___

6 Something that gets in the way or stops something happening

h ___ ___ ___ ___ a ___ c ___

7 A hard layer of protection against attack

___ ___ ___ ___ ___ r

8 A group of young animals born at the same time to the same mother

___ ___ t ___ ___ ___

9 Almost the same as

___ ___ ___ ___ l ___ r

10 An intention to hurt or harm someone

___ h r ___ ___ ___

11 No longer in existence

___ x ___ ___ ___ c ___

12 An animal that preys on others

p ___ ___ ___ ___ ___ t ___ r

Puzzle 7 — Wordsearches

In these two wordsearches, 20 words are hidden (ten in each puzzle). They are all taken from Test 21. The first wordsearch contains words describing the setting and the second contains words connected to the meteor.

```
F  I  C  D  E  Y  R  V  M  G  Q  F  F  B  N
W  O  K  T  L  W  I  P  I  O  C  N  Z  O  N
I  P  O  T  H  L  Z  Z  Q  X  Z  S  U  C  X
U  B  N  T  L  G  L  D  O  R  D  E  U  O  J
G  A  U  A  H  A  I  R  U  M  E  M  Y  L  D
A  F  G  R  F  I  Y  R  A  O  D  S  W  D  Y
R  E  K  K  Z  V  L  B  B  U  O  Z  Q  U  Q
S  V  A  L  L  E  Y  L  H  N  O  A  A  E  I
D  G  Z  S  Q  M  V  Q  S  T  W  P  W  S  D
R  E  N  I  U  Z  T  I  L  A  C  G  E  O  Q
C  Q  N  R  H  N  J  V  T  I  L  P  M  I  J
L  T  S  C  C  S  N  G  F  N  O  R  O  J  F
G  N  I  N  R  O  M  Y  Z  L  U  I  R  Q  U
K  I  E  V  O  E  A  H  S  B  A  R  T  E  O
```

_____
_____
_____
_____
_____
_____
_____
_____
_____
_____

```
S  E  F  T  H  U  N  D  E  R  C  L  A  P  S
N  I  L  I  E  J  K  U  N  C  Q  K  G  T  D
O  X  A  T  R  N  N  O  B  M  X  W  S  Q  O
I  Y  S  I  H  E  I  L  M  F  Q  T  C  A  Z
T  Y  H  I  T  T  B  C  P  S  M  O  K  E  J
A  D  E  P  A  P  F  A  A  I  G  D  A  F  S
R  T  D  R  J  Q  R  M  L  C  R  R  B  J  H
B  K  B  F  O  J  B  N  C  L  R  R  B  J  H
I  I  W  B  G  U  S  T  R  H  W  X  D  F  X
V  P  A  H  R  Z  R  A  E  V  A  W  R  I  A
U  K  C  N  A  I  G  K  D  V  X  R  X  C  X
O  Y  I  M  P  E  G  F  N  R  A  O  R  F  I
G  N  L  V  Z  D  M  Y  U  C  M  O  Q  R  B
G  S  H  A  T  T  E  R  E  D  K  O  A  G  N
```

_____
_____
_____
_____
_____
_____
_____
_____
_____
_____

Puzzle 8

Missing Words

Read the following paragraphs and add words from the box to each space so that the paragraphs make sense.

solitary   mating   flexibility   solving problems

wise   locate   flight   significantly

unusual   binocular   active during the night

Owls

Owls are _____ birds. They are nocturnal, which means

they are _____. They are mostly _____,

except during the _____ season. They have

_____ vision, which allows them to see more and helps

them to _____ prey. They have special feathers adapted

for silent _____.

They have fourteen vertebrae, which allows _____ in

their neck. Mythology says that owls are _____, but

in fact studies show that although they are adept at hunting, they may be

_____ worse at _____ than

parrots or crows.

Puzzle 9 · Odd Words Out

Each list of words has **TWO** that do not fit. Find the odd words to create List 5 and List 6. Remember: all the words in each list have a similar meaning. At least one word in each list is taken from a text in this book.

List 1	List 2	List 3	List 4
tradition	lush	alarming	ludicrous
giant	verdant	frightening	rapid
custom	abundant	preposterous	fast
ritual	huge	worrying	speedy
practice	thriving	scary	quick
absurd	prolific	terrifying	brisk
habit	luxuriant	enormous	vast
routine	ridiculous	shocking	prompt

List 5

_____

_____

_____

_____

List 6

_____

_____

_____

_____

Key words

adjective a word that is used to describe or give more information about a noun; may come before a noun or after the verb 'to be', for example *the tall tree; The tree was tall.*

adverb a word that gives more information about a verb; usually refers to the time or manner in which something is done, for example *He walked to school slowly. She often rides her bike.*

alliteration when adjacent words, or words that are close to each other, begin with the same letter or sound, for example *The wild wind whistled.*

antonym a word that means the opposite of another word, for example *hot* and *cold* are a pair of antonyms

deduce make a reasoned conclusion about something, based on the information given in a text

explain make something clear and give a reason, using your own words, rather than just quoting a section of text

metaphor a kind of figurative language where something is described as being something else, which it is not, for example *Life is a roller coaster.*

noun a word that is a person, place, object or feeling, for example *child, school, book, happiness*

personification a kind of figurative language where something is described as if it were a person, for example *The flowers danced in the breeze and smiled as they reached their faces to the sun.*

simile a kind of figurative language where something is compared to something else, usually using 'as' or 'like' to make the comparison, for example *The ice sparkled like diamonds.*

synonym a word that means the same as or similar to another word, for example *pretty, beautiful* and *attractive* are all synonyms

verb a word that conveys an action or a state of being; sometimes called a 'doing' word; can be in the past, present or future tense, for example *He baked a cake; The children are hungry.*

Progress chart

How did you do? Fill in your score below and shade in the corresponding boxes to compare your progress across the different tests.

50% 100% 50% 100%

Test 1, p4 Score: _____ /12

Test 2, p6 Score: _____ /13

Test 3, p8 Score: _____ /11

Test 4, p10 Score: _____ /11

Test 5, p12 Score: _____ /17

Test 6, p14 Score: _____ /10

Test 7, p16 Score: _____ /14

Test 8, p18 Score: _____ /9

Test 9, p20 Score: _____ /13

Test 10, p22 Score: _____ /11

Test 11, p24 Score: _____ /14

Test 12, p26 Score: _____ /13

Test 13, p28 Score: _____ /11

Test 14, p30 Score: _____ /15

Test 15, p32 Score: _____ /10

Test 16, p34 Score: _____ /8

Test 17, p36 Score: _____ /10

Test 18, p38 Score: _____ /16

Test 19, p60 Score: _____ /14

Test 20, p62 Score: _____ /12

Test 21, p64 Score: _____ /10

Test 22, p66 Score: _____ /7

Test 23, p68 Score: _____ /8

Test 24, p70 Score: _____ /14

Test 25, p72 Score: _____ /10

Test 26, p74 Score: _____ /9

Test 27, p76 Score: _____ /14

Test 28 p78 Score: _____ /10

Test 29, p80 Score: _____ /10

Test 30, p82 Score: _____ /9

Test 31, p84 Score: _____ /12